THE FOUNDATIONS AND MATHEMATICAL MODELS OF OPERATIONS RESEARCH WITH EXTENSIONS TO THE CRIMINAL JUSTICE SYSTEM

HAIG EDWARD BOHIGIAN

John Jay College of Criminal Justice

A Ph.D. dissertation in the School of Education of New York University under a sponsoring committee consisting of:
Professor Stephen S. Willoughby, Chairman
Professor Herbert Schwartz
Professor H. Harry Giles
Professor Irwin Greenberg, Technical Advisor

HV8665
.B59
1971

Library of Congress Catalogue Card Number: 75 - 186274

Printed and published in the United States of America by:

THE GAZETTE PRESS, INC.
69 Warburton Avenue
Yonkers, New York 10701

PREFACE

This dissertation is a direct outgrowth of the
researcher's experience in operations research (OR)
consultation work, and the development of an OR
curriculum at the John Jay College of Criminal
Justice.[1] The study is intended to provide a means
of incorporating OR courses into the curricula and
training programs of the growing list of educational
institutions, governmental agencies, and private
organizations that are dedicated in part or in whole
to the study of criminal justice (CJ). Additionally,
mathematics educators should conclude that although
OR is traditionally taught in graduate schools,
most of the OR models discussed herein can be taught
at the secondary or the undergraduate college level.

The need for an OR study of this type was first
identified by Alex M. Mood,[2] a study proposal was
spelled out by Irwin Greenberg,[3] and a total overview
of the potential OR study areas in CJ was discussed by

---

1 Haig Bohigian, "OR Education for Criminal Justice
Professionals," (paper presented at the 38th national
meeting of the Operations Research Society of America,
Detroit, Mich., October 30, 1970).

2 Alex M. Mood, "Diversification of Operations Research,"
Operations Research, 13 (March-April, 1965), 169-178.

3 Irwin Greenberg, "A New Application of Operations
Research," Operations Research, 8 (May-June, 1960),
423-424.

Alfred Blumstein.[1] From the CJ point of view, the
need for a study of this type was identified by
Frank D. Day,[2] A. C. Germann,[3] and Norval Morris.[4]

The study is designed to be of educational
value in the areas of mathematics, OR, and CJ.
It indirectly answers the challenge posed in the
Cambridge Conference Report,[5] as to whether the
methods of OR can be incorporated into the mathematics
curricula before college. It demonstrates some
specific ways of incorporating OR methods into the
education of CJ professionals, considered to be still
in its infancy by Donald H. Riddle.[6] It addresses

1 Alfred Blumstein, "Outline of a Future Research
and Development Program," in Law Enforcement Science
and Technology II, ed. by S. I. Cohn (Chicago: IIT
Research Institute, 1969), 57-60.

2 Frank D. Day, "Administration of Criminal Justice:
An Educational Design in Higher Education," Journal
of Criminal Law, Criminology, and Police Science,
56 (December, 1965), 540-544.

3 A. C. Germann, "Education and Professional Law
Enforcement," Journal of Criminal Law, Criminology,
and Police Science, 58 (June, 1967), 603-609.

4 Norval Morris, "Crime Prevention and Professional
Education," in Law Enforcement Science and Technology I,
ed. by S. A. Yefsky (Washington, D. C.: Thompson Book
Co., 1967), 63-65.

5 Cambridge Conference, Report on the Correlation
of Science and Mathematics in the Schools, Goals for
the Correlation of Elementary Science and Mathematics
(Boston: Houghton Mifflin Co., 1969), 95.

6 Donald H. Riddle, "How Do You Educate Police?
'Like Anyone Else'," University Magazine (Princeton
University, Spring, 1969 issue), 13-16.

the deficiency, pointed out by Seth Bonder,[1] that
most OR programs teach models and model solutions,
and completely ignore the art of how to develop
and apply new OR models to virgin areas.

The dissertation was undertaken to provide,
in a single source, the foundations and mathematical
models of OR most applicable to the analysis of the
CJ system, but currently available only in diverse
sources. The mathematical models of OR selected for
inclusion in this study were chosen so as to maximize
their potential usage in the analyses of the CJ system,
and to minimize the potential apprehensions of those
CJ professionals who have had a limited or uncomfort-
able exposure to mathematical methods.

---

1 Seth Bonder, "Needs in Operations Research
Education," (paper presented at the 37th national
meeting of the Operations Research Society of
America, Washington, D. C., April 22, 1970).

ACKNOWLEDGEMENT

I am indebted to the administration,
faculty, and students of the John Jay College of
Criminal Justice, CUNY, for having had the
opportunity to apply my research in a realistic
setting. A special debt is owed to my Chairman,
Professor Alexander Joseph, Division of Science
and Mathematics, and to Professor Leo Loughrey,
Chairman, Division of Law and Police Science, who
had the foresight to encourage the start of an OR
program for CJ professionals. I am thankful for
the assistance extended by Professor Edgar Lavoie
of the Law and Police Science Division during the
OR curriculum development, and our team teaching
efforts.

None of the research into the literature
would have been possible without the excellent
facilities and cooperative staffs of the following
libraries: John Jay, New York City Public, M.I.T.,
Columbia Engineering, New York University Engineering;
and particularly the Library of the Courant Institute
of Mathematical Sciences.

I am thankful for the inspiration of
Professor Morris Kline's personal counsel which
led me to pursue the doctorate. I gladly acknowledge
the vital role Prof. Janice Gorn played in developing

the research design.

I am appreciative of the efforts and sacrifices
made by my Sponsoring Committee during the course
of my studies. To the Chairman, Professor Stephen
Willoughby whose precise suggestions were carefully
aimed to perfect the study. To Professor H. Harry
Giles, whose advice was needed to bring out the
humanity of the study. To Professor Herbert Schwartz,
whose encouragement made the writing so much easier.
And to Professor Irwin Greenberg, whose expertise
served to clear up many inaccuracies.

The efforts of Robert Levine, in proof reading
the dissertation draft, are greatly appreciated.
I extend total reverence to the typist, Connie Engle,
who had to wade through a maze of corrections and
changes under severe time deadlines, and still managed
to produce a beautiful manuscript.

Finally, the dissertation is dedicated to my
wife, Valerie, who gave me the incentive and strength
to complete the dissertation, and who knows how
lifesaving OR can be.

Haig E. Bohigian

June, 1971

ABSTRACT

The objective of this dissertation is to bridge the communication gap between most operations research (OR) and criminal justice (CJ) professionals. The foundations and mathematical models of OR are presented as a viable means of dealing with the magnitude and the complexities of the CJ system. The OR analyst and the mathematics educator are introduced to the variety of problems and challenges in the CJ system that are in need of study.

Part I examines the foundations of OR. The roots of OR are traced to Biblical and ancient Greek sources. Various claims over the founding of OR are discussed. The nature of OR is exhibited in the many definitions appearing in the literature. A synthesized definition of OR is presented. OR studies are characterized uniquely by the 10 M criterion: the manipulation of mathematical models to measure the management of men, machines, methods, and money in their milieu.

OR emerged quite naturally as a perfection of the scientific method. Aspects of several past scientific achievements are shown to be the precursors of modern OR. The important contributions of Babbage, Taylor, Erlang, Edison, Lanchester, Levinson, and Schneider to the development of OR are discussed.

The origins of OR are traced principally to applications
in business and warfare. The acceleration of OR into
a separate discipline was accomplished during World
War II, and some historical notes on this period
are included.

The philosophy of OR is summarized through an
examination of the ten key steps essential to all
OR studies. Case histories with implications for
CJ are presented along with each step. Potential and
actual pitfalls and fallacies in OR modeling are
discussed along with their implications for CJ studies.

Part II develops the concept and nature of
mathematical modeling and its limitations, along with
a brief historical sketch of each model discussed.
Qualitative methods using formula, black box, Venn
diagram, and flow chart models are developed and
applied to various aspects of the CJ system.

The assignment algorithm is presented in detail
with specific instructions for determining the
minimum number of covering lines, and for finding
all alternative optimal solutions. The assignment
algorithm is applied to the administration of a
forensic science laboratory, and is extended to
consider a new method of assignment based on weighted
multiple criteria.

The transportation algorithm is presented with detailed instructions designed to obtain a nearly optimal initial solution, to test for optimality, and to display alternate optimal solutions. Applications are demonstrated to the transfer of inmates, and the refueling of police motorized units.

The Johnson algorithm for two and three stage sequencing problems is applied to forensic science laboratory procedures, and District Attorney operations. A new algorithm for minimizing interim delays in the second and third stages is developed, along with a method to determine alternate optimal solutions.

A complete set of formulas for analyzing M/M/C queueing systems is presented, and applied to the operations of a criminal court system. A table of key queueing parameters is displayed as a function of a system's utilization factor.

Due to the stochastic and dynamic nature of the CJ system the only method for solving certain of its problems is through simulation. The Monte Carlo method is applied to predict the new service call distributions that might develop by combining various existing police precincts into proposed new ones.

Opportunities for further research and application of OR to the CJ system are discussed. A presentation of CJ problems that are potentially amenable to OR analysis is offered.

TABLE OF CONTENTS

PART I.   THE FOUNDATIONS OF

OPERATIONS RESEARCH

Chapter

Chapter

LIST OF TABLES

LIST OF ILLUSTRATIONS

PART I

THE FOUNDATIONS OF OPERATIONS RESEARCH

CHAPTER I

THE NATURE OF OPERATIONS RESEARCH

Descriptions and Definitions of Operations Research

Even though operational or operations research (OR)
has been referred to as a new branch of science or
philosophy, a new form of engineering or mathematics,
and a new level of research or decision making, as of
yet "there is no general agreement on the definition
of operational or operations research..."[1] In fact,
M. G. Kendall has claimed that subjects such as OR
cannot be adequately defined by definitions.[2] The
attempt to define OR is complicated by its unique blend
of theory and experiment which has been quite successful
in influencing the policy decisions of management in a
wide variety of fields.

The name OR was coined about thirty years ago for
a discipline that had been developing under a series of
aliases for centuries.[3] Since that time, many OR

1 J. W. Mayne, "Operational Research and the Design of
Experiments," Operations Research (hereinafter, Opns.
Res.), 4 (February, 1956), 113.

2 M. G. Kendall, "The Teaching of Operational Research,"
Operational Research Quarterly 9 (December, 1958), 266.

3 Philip Morse, "The History and Development of Operations
Research," in The Challenge to Systems Analysis: Public
Policy and Social Change, ed. by Grace J. Kelleher (New
York: John Wiley & Sons, Inc., 1970), 21.

analysts have tried, unsuccessfully, to provide a
universally acceptable definition of OR. The formulation of a concise and accurate definition is especially
difficult since OR tends to be subjectively described,
diversely applied, and pragmatically developed.

In searching for an appropriate definition of OR
that includes the gamut of its activities, many OR
analysts have selected a simple characterization which,
while originally offered in a serious vein, in retrospect
has become an amusingly inadequate description of OR.
One of the more barren of these definitions was cited,
without credit, by Robert F. Rinehart: "OR is what
operations-research workers do."[1] Sir Charles Goodeve
labeled OR as quantitative common-sense.[2] Thomas A. Cowan
described OR as, "... perhaps, the first attempt in
the history of science to socialize scientific method
on a planned and conscious basis."[3] Probably the most
open-ended description was that OR is at present undefined but will become defined in time by the subject
matter appearing in the literature.[4]

---

1 Robert F. Rinehart, "Threats to the Growth of Operations Research in Business and Industry," Opns. Res., 2
(August, 1954), 231.

2 Sir Charles Goodeve, "Operational Research," Nature
161, (March 13, 1948), 377.

3 Thomas A. Cowan, "Social Implications of Operations
Research," Opns. Res., 3 (August, 1955), 341.

4 Philip M. Morse, "Trends in Operations Research,"
Opns. Res., 1 (August, 1953), 159.

The search for an appropriate description of OR
activities has produced a few lighthearted gems which
at face value are seemingly whimsical, but nevertheless
are frequently quite accurate. For example, the characterization that OR estimates destructive effects and
plans destructive policy was attributed to Sir Henry
Dale.[1] The quip that OR is the medication which can
cure a sick business or keep a healthy one ahead of the
competition,[2] merely described a potential result without identifying the methodology needed to obtain it.
And finally, many an analyst must admit, however
reluctantly, that often, OR is the art of providing
bad solutions to problems that might otherwise be given
worse solutions.[3]

The most widely quoted definition appears in what
is generally regarded as the first OR textbook:

> Operations research is a scientific method of
> providing executive departments with a quantita-
> tive basis for decisions regarding the operations
> under their control.[4]

However, this definition should be credited to Sir
Charles Kittel who put forth a similar one for

---

1 "Operational Research in War and Peace," Nature, 160
(November 15, 1947), 560.

2 W. T. M. Johnson, "Why Operations Research?" Opns. Res.,
3 (February, 1955), 104.

3 Thomas L. Saaty, Mathematical Methods of Operations
Research (New York: McGraw-Hill Book Co., 1959), 3.

4 Philip M. Morse and George E. Kimball, Methods of
Operations Research (1st ed. rev., Cambridge, Mass.:
The M.I.T. Press, 1970), 1.

operational research[1] which was later modified by
Sir Charles Goodeve[2] to the exact form quoted above
at a conference organized by the Committee of Directors
of Research Associations held in Ashorne Hill, England,
January 13-14, 1948.[3]

The previous definition when combined with the
description that OR provides "... a framework that
permits the judgement of experts in numerous sub-fields
to be combined to yield results which transcend any
individual judgement,"[4] forms a logical basis for the
following definition:

> Operations research is the application of scien-
> tific method by interdisciplinary teams to
> problems involving the control of organized
> (man-machine) systems so as to provide solutions
> which best serve the purposes of the organization
> as a whole.[5]

It seems reasonable to conclude that the previous
definitions when combined with the characterization of
OR as the study of a dynamic sequence of events or
operations, led the Operational Research Society of

1 Sir Charles Kittel, "The Nature and Development of
Operations Research," Science, 105 (February 7, 1947), 150.

2 "The Meaning and Function of Operational Research,"
in Operational Research in Practice, ed. by Max Davies
and Michel Verhulst (London: Pergamon Press, 1958), 2.

3 "Operational Research in the Research Associations,"
Nature, 161 (April 17, 1948), 584.

4 Charles Hitch,"An Appreciation of Systems Analysis,"
Opns. Res. 3 (November, 1955), 481.

5 Russell Ackoff and Maurice Sasieni, Fundamentals of
Operations Research (New York: John Wiley & Sons, Inc.,
1968), 6.

Great Britain to adopt a standard definition of OR
which follows; an accord which the Operations Research
Society of America (ORSA) has been, as yet, unable to
attain.

> Operational research is the attack of modern
> science on complex problems arising in the
> direction and management of large systems of
> men, machines, materials and money in industry,
> business, government, and defense. Its distinc-
> tive approach is to develop a scientific model
> of the system, incorporating measurements of
> factors such as chance and risk, with which to
> predict and compare the outcomes of alternative
> decisions, strategies or controls. The purpose
> is to help management determine its policy and
> actions scientifically.[1]

The preceding collection of descriptions and definitions when viewed collectively with the presumptuous
position cited, without credit, by Rinehart that "OR is
simultaneously Industrial Engineering, Statistics,
Quality Control, Market Analysis, Civil Engineering,
Applied Mathematics, Applied Physics, Applied Psychology,
and Econometrics,"[2] tends to reflect the infancy of OR
as a discipline, and the early insecurity of some OR
practitioners. This view was supported by W. N. Jessop:

> Operational Research is still young and self-
> conscious, it is therefore very much concerned
> with what it is, how it came to be what it is, and
> what its standing is in comparison with other sciences
> -- indeed, whether it is a science at all.[3]

---

1 Stafford Beer, Decision and Control (London: John
Wiley & Sons, Inc., 1966), 92.

2 Rinehart, 231.

3 William N. Jessop, "Operational Research Methods:
What Are They?" Operational Research Quarterly, 7
(June, 1956), 49.

The search for a universal, unequivocal, and
definitive definition of OR may, paradoxically, involve
the methods of OR for resolution, or even may be futile
if OR were considered as an undefined phrase in a logical
construct. Whatever apparent circularity or difficulty
exists in defining OR can be alleviated by substituting
more flexible criteria instead of the rigid ones
necessary for a definition in the pure mathematical
sense. To this end, and for the purposes of this study,
OR will be defined as follows.

> OR is an interdisciplinary, scientific approach
> to the solution of problems that involve the
> complex, dynamic, and subjective interaction of
> men, methods, and systems which are generally
> unyielding to exact solution by purely analytic
> or trial-and-error techniques. By using mathe-
> matical modeling as a primary resource, OR
> methodology is designed to quantify and bound
> these problems within the framework of certain
> implied or specified constraints, measures,
> objectives, and variables, so as to seek optimal
> operating controls, decisions, levels, and
> solutions.

The Naming and Claiming of Operations Research

OR type studies have functioned as unheralded
orphans of the scientific method for centuries, and
many researchers before and during the twentieth
century did work of the OR sort but referred to it by
other names. Specifically, OR has assumed many aliases
such as, time and motion study, work study, business
consultation, industrial engineering, management science,
systems analysis, operations analysis, and systems
engineering. Once named, OR lost any adverse stigmas

it may have had, and became a coveted child that several scientists were to claim they sired. In fact, "probably, on balance, the name [OR] has helped, instead of hindered, in spreading the idea."[1]

It is generally acknowledged that OR was first formally organized, officially sanctioned, and widely used in the United Kingdom where it is known as operational research rather than operations research. "The term operational research was specifically coined, by A. P. Rowe, to describe the activities of a small section of the Air Ministry Research Station at Bawdsey in the years 1937-39."[2] The word "operational" served to differentiate the Bawsdey section work from the research and development work being done elsewhere on radar. Also, it was employed to avoid confusion with the term "operations" which had a specific connotation in the Armed Services in connection with military logistics and strategy. Actually, the somewhat earlier and independent work of B. G. Dickins on methods of fighter plane interception "... was, equally well, operational research although it was not, at the time, called by that name."[3]

This viewpoint on the origin of studies labeled as OR was challenged by Sir Robert Watson-Watt, who claimed

---

1 Morse, "The History and Development of Operations Research," 25.

2 Eric C. Williams, "Reflections on Operations Research," Opns. Res., 2 (November, 1954), 441.

3 Ibid.

that he launched the first two OR studies for the
British military in 1937.[1] In fact, he claimed far
more than the mere naming of OR. "I believe myself to
have been a first and true 'inventor' of operational
research, which was certainly high among the instruments
of victory in every theater of war."[2] The former claim
is somewhat substantiated by Philip M. Morse who stated
that "... one or the other or both (and it is uncertain
which) Sir Robert Watson-Watt and A. P. Rowe coined the
term 'operational research section' ..."[3] However,
even Watson-Watt admitted that: "I think it was about
mid-1940 when I first suggested the names Operational
Research and Operational Research Section for these
rapidly extending activities,"[4] whereas the term OR
seemed to have been already in common usage by 1939.

As to the latter claim that he invented OR, there
seems to be little evidence to support his allegation.
The only apparent OR contribution, in writing, by
Watson-Watt is a report dated March 27, 1942 that he
presented to the U. S. Secretary of War and Navy, based
on an inspection mission of the Pacific Coast and the

1 Sir Robert Watson-Watt, Three Steps to Victory
(London: Odhams Press, 1957), 203.

2 Sir Robert Watson-Watt, The Pulse of Radar (An Autobiography) (New York: The Dial Press, 1959), 319.

3 Morse, "The History and Development of Operations
Research," 22.

4 Watson-Watt, The Pulse of Radar (An Autobiography),
321.

Panama Canal Zone, which urged the advantages of beginning OR studies in these areas, particularly as they pertained to defensive radar operations.[1] P. M. S. Blackett,[2] an extensive contributor to OR during World War II, does credit Watson-Watt, along with Sir Henry Tizard, A. P. Rowe, and G. H. Larnder as being among the scientists whose ideas were paramount in formulating the ideas of the British use of OR during World War II. Sir Solly Zuckerman claimed that Watson-Watt introduced OR "... into the British military sphere, as a necessary corollary to the development of radar from a laboratory phenomenon to the sensory system on which a modern air force relies ..."[3]

With respect to the coined term "operations research," there seems to be no controversy. It was originated by Morse, an early pioneer in OR studies during World War II. Morse has continued to make outstanding contributions to the OR literature, but has humbly observed that:

> ...I sometimes wonder whether my most lasting influence on the whole field will not be the substitution of an 's' (operations) for an 'al' (operational) in half of the writings on the subject. I am not sure now what caused me to do this: maybe it was an unconscious rebellion against the niceties of English grammar.[4]

---

1 Watson-Watt, The Pulse of Radar (An Autobiography), 321-324.

2 P. M. S. Blackett, "Operational Research," The Advancement of Science, V (April, 1948), 27.

3 Sir Solly Zuckerman, "The Need for Operational Research," in Davies and Verhulst, 7.

4 Morse, "The History and Development of Operations Research," 25.

A somewhat different justification was proposed by
Watson-Watt. "I suspect that the substitution of 's'
for 'al' was due to an amendment to Clemenceau's
view that war is too serious to be left to soldiers;
perhaps war was thought to be too serious to be
entrusted to civilians!"[1]

The Ancient Roots of Operations Research

OR has been regarded by some, as a new, different
or magical discipline. But as Joseph F. McCloskey, a
trained historian and contributor to the OR literature
has observed, OR is actually a natural development
appropriate to our times.[2] OR has emerged from ancient
roots in a manner reminiscent of the world historic
concept of Hegel. It would be non-productive and almost
certainly impossible to pin-point the first recorded use
of techniques that resemble modern OR procedures.
Nevertheless, by modern standards, those ancient scientific
activities that involved the interplay of men, machines,
and methods also might be classified as early OR case
histories.

It would not be difficult to conjecture therefore,
that such great architectural and engineering marvels

1 Watson-Watt, The Pulse of Radar (An Autobiography),
325.

2 Joseph F. McCloskey, "The Training for Operations
Research," in Operations Research, notes by J. Hoagbin
(Ann Arbor: The University of Michigan Press, 1957), 147.

as the Egyptian Pyramids, the Chinese Great Wall, and
the Roman Aqueduct System involved the use of some OR
procedures. Certainly, ancient astronomers and high
priests, who using a " ... prior 2,000 years of observation, could predict many astronomical events with a
degree of precision of about one part in a million,"[1]
and thereby being able to subjugate the masses by
accurately foretelling eclipses and floods, should be
mentioned as among the earliest practitioners of OR.

In terms of early military applications, it has
been claimed that OR was used on a small scale by the
Athenians and the Syracusans in the Peloponnesian Wars
(431 to 404 B.C.), as told by Thucydides.[2] But to
describe for example, the sound military tactics of
Demosthenes or Ariston as related by Thucydides,[3]
as good OR seems a bit overgenerous. If this were the
case, then Hannibal must be credited with using some
OR procedures in guiding his armies over the Alps, and
the use of the Trojan Horse by the Athenians might be
considered as a combined use of tactical and psychological weaponry in the best OR tradition. Additionally,

---

1 Ellis A. Johnson, "The Long-Range Future of Operational
Research," Opns. Res., 8 (January-February, 1960), 3.

2 Hitch, "An Appreciation of Systems Analysis," 466.

3 The Complete Writings of Thucydides: The Peloponnesian
War, trans. by R. Crawley, (New York: The Modern Library,
1934), 227 and 422.

the Macedonian military phalanx devised by Phillip of
Macedon, and perfected by his son, Alexander the Great,
which was unbeatable in its time, has been described
as a self-contained system, designed by OR type trade-
offs between its great strength and its need for greater
striking power.[1]

The Old Testament probably contained the first clear
reference to OR consultation. Moses is warned by Jethro,
his father-in-law, that his organizational methods in
judging his people are inefficient, and that "... thou
art not able to perform it thyself alone."[2] Thus,
"Jethro here appears as the prototype of the counselor
in organization, and the principles he advocates, sub-
division of work and selection of the right assistants,
are basic in modern management."[3] It should be noted
that this same message is related to Moses by God in
Numbers 11: 14-17.

A good case can be made for the claim that the concept of controlled trade-offs, so essential to OR
methods such as linear programming, was first propounded
by Plato. Plato claimed that the man who pursued
intellect would reap the highest rewards and approach

---

1 Handel Davies and K. E. Silman, "Some Examples of
Systems Analysis," in Davies and Verhulst, 36.

2 Exodus 18: 18-19.

3 "Notes to Exodus," in The Dartmouth Bible, R. B.
Chamberlin and H. Feldman (2nd ed.; Boston: Houghton
Mifflin Co., 1961), 114.

the Kingdom of Heaven, whereas the man who sought
immediate rewards would never gain them with any degree
of permanence. "Running through The Republic we therefore encounter an underlying theme based upon an optimum
performance resulting from a controlled compromise".[1]

A similar theme involving a trade-off in the
privileges a citizen must forgo within the composition
of a State, is found in Aristotle.[2] Additionally,
The New Testament indicated that the pursuit of an
optimum achievement such as salvation, must be accomplished through the controlled compromises of faith and
the rejection of worldly possessions.[3] However, perhaps
to the envy of many an OR analyst, Jesus, through divine
intervention, was able to solve many "management problems"
such as the conversion of water to wine,[4] without having
to consider the trade-off of compromises, or the limita-
tion of constraints.

Archimedes (circa 287-212 B.C.), was undoubtedly
the first practitioner of OR in a form prescient of
modern methods, and may, with some merit, be considered
as the founder of the subject. It was not Archimedes'

---

1 Earl of Halsbury, "From Plato to the Linear Program,"
Opns. Res., 3 (August, 1955), 244.
2 Aristotle, Politics, Book III, Chapter 1.
3 Consult, St. Matthew, 6: 19-34.
4 St. John, 2: 1-11.

outstanding classical mathematical and scientific
works that ranked him among the early contributors
to OR, but rather his ability to apply this knowledge
along with his engineering and inventive skills to the
complex logistics and tactics of warfare involving men
and machines. Because "Archimedes, like Plato, held
that it was undesirable for a philosopher to seek to
apply the results of science to any practical use,..."[1]
he did not deign to leave any notes on the design or
operation of the various war-machines he invented. Were
it not for the early historians, most of his practical
achievements in the OR vein might not have been recorded.

Archimedes' first great "OR type feat" was achieved
by designing compound pulleys for the famous ship
Syracosia, that King Hiero had built for his colleague
Ptolemy, which would allow one man to launch and operate
the fully laden vessel where formerly it had required
the concerted efforts of a large band of men.[2] King
Hiero was so impressed that he requested Archimedes to
set about devising means of defense and offense against
the Roman siege of Syracuse, the capital of the "neutral"

1 Philip E. B. Jourdain, "The Nature of Mathematics,"
in The World of Mathematics, Vol. 1, notes and comments
by James R. Newman (New York: Simon and Schuster, 1956),
15.

2 B. L. van der Waerden, Science Awakening, trans. by
Arnold Dresden (New York: John Wiley & Sons, Inc., 1963),
209.

Greek colony of Sicily, during the second Punic War
(218-201 B.C.). Thus, it was "... Archimedes [who]
did the first operational research by advising the
King of Syracuse on his combat strategy."[1]

Archimedes, an amateur at war, was pitting his
genius against the experienced Roman general, Marcellus.
However, Marcellus' attacks upon Syracuse, though "...
furnished with all sorts of arms and missiles, and ...
relying on the abundance and magnificience of his
preparations, and on his own previous glory [turned
out to be]... but trifles for Archimedes and his
machines."[2] So thorough was the disguise and the
execution of his techniques of warfare, that mere
suggestion was sufficient to cause mass hysteria among
the Roman soldiers, so that "... if they saw a little
piece of rope or of wood projecting over the wall, they
cried, 'There it is, Archimedes is training some engine
upon us,' and fled."[3] Archimedes succeeded in prolong-
ing the siege of Syrcause to two years before it was
taken; and Marcellus, the long-frustrated Roman
commander bemoaned: "Shall we not cease fighting against
this geometrical Briareus,... who outdoes all the
hundred-handed monsters of fable in hurling so many
missiles against us all at once?"[4]

---

1 Beer, 15.
2 Plutarch, "Marcellus," in Newman, Vol. 1, 180.
3 Ibid., 183.
4 Ibid.

The OR accomplishments of this seventy year old
mathematician during the siege of Syracuse were no
doubt exaggerated to some extent by the historians
Polybius, Livy, and Plutarch, and later were glorified
to the status of fiction by writers such as Galen,
Lucian and Tzetzes. Ironically, Archimedes was killed
while paying too much attention to theoretical pursuits,
and not enough attention to pragmatic concerns -- an
unpardonable pitfall for any modern OR analyst, but
hardly of any consequence to this great genius of
mathematics and science. One version of his death
depicts him so intently pondering the solution to a
problem drawn in the sand, that he was summarily executed
for failure to heed the instructions of a soldier of
the invading Roman legions which finally overcame the
Syracusan defenses.[1]

---

1 Plutarch, 185.

CHAPTER II

THE ORIGINS OF OPERATIONS RESEARCH

The Scientific Method and Operations Research

It is not difficult to study the development of
the scientific method, and to find therein, parallels
and roots of the development of OR. At present, it is
not entirely clear what the relationship is between the
two. There is the extreme position that "the need for
extensibility of constructs puts into science the
expansive drive by which it spreads over adjacent
territory, tending ultimately to cover all experience."[1]
There is also the extreme but contrasting position that,
"OR can be thought of as the scientific study of the
process by which men, materials, and know-how combine in
every human enterprise."[2] Consequently if distinctions
are to be made, a good deal of selectivity must be
exercised in choosing those historical aspects of the
development of the scientific method that appear to be
most germane to the development of modern OR.

----

1 Henry Margenau, "The Competence and Limitations of
Scientific Method," Opns. Res., 3 (May, 1955), 141.
2 Nigel J. Hopkins, "Operations Research in Relation
to the Human-Enterprise Process," Opns. Res., 4 (June,
1956), 360.

The modern OR think-tank, as exemplified by the
Rand Corporation and Herman Kahn's Hudson Institute,
is dedicated to pooling the mental resources of men
and computers to study system problems within the
framework of the scientific method as updated by OR.
The first think-tank may have originated with the
ancient Greeks, and with Plato's Academy in particular.
Even the medieval alchemists may be ranked as among the
first think-tank staffers, because of the abundant
output of chemical discoveries uncovered during their
tireless but unsuccessful search for a chemical
synthesis of gold from the more plentiful elements.

Leonardo da Vinci (1452-1519), embodied the true
Renaissance spirit of the all-around man of multiple
interests and talents that ranged from art to zoology.
He applied his mastery of many disciplines in a manner
that anticipated the interchange between the scientific
method and modern OR, because he was able to view complex
reality from many vantage points without falling victim
to the potential dangers of suboptimization. In many
ways da Vinci would have made an ideal OR analyst
because he "... was a genius of bold and original thought,
a man of action as well as contemplation, at once an
artist and an engineer..."[1] who found it as interesting
to design the sewers used in the Lombard canal system

1 Carl B. Boyer, A History of Mathematics (New York:
John Wiley & Sons, Inc., 1968), 308.

as he did to detail the sketches of contemplated submarines and aeroplanes.

As Francis Bacon did later, da Vinci distrusted that book knowledge devoid from the realities of experience which was professed so dogmatically by the scholars of their day. By helping to discard the metaphysical constraints of Aristotelian philosophy, da Vinci anticipated the use of experimental determination and verification as a vital part of the scientific method. His principal tools were patient observation, exhaustive study, and meticulous sketching of nearly everything within sight. Although da Vinci relied heavily on experience and observation, he insisted on striking a balance between theory and practice in his work in a manner that anticipated trade-off concepts used in the search for optimality in modern OR. Da Vinci's fertile mind constantly caused him to search out new challenges before old ones were completely solved -- an undesirable trait for an OR analyst, but hardly a deterrent to his productive genius.

Although da Vinci pioneered the use of experience in scientific studies, Morris Kline noted that "... prior to Galileo the use of experience to build scientific doctrine was fumbling and without direction."[1] Galileo

---

1 Morris Kline, Mathematics and the Physical World (New York: Thomas Y. Crowell, 1959), 196.

Galilei (1564-1642), probably was first to demonstrate,
that in addition to metaphysical considerations, the
collection of quantitative data, the quantitative
analysis of data, and the conducting of experiments,
all of which form essential parts of modern scientific
method and OR methodology, were necessary to scholarly
studies. Additionally, Galileo was among the first
scientists to take advantage of technological advances
to enhance his work, just as some modern OR analysts
have formed an inseparable bond with the computer.

> The telescope made sunspots and Jupiter's moons
> a part of Galileo's science, just as particle
> accelerators and the mathematical machinery of
> quantum mechanics bring the interior of the atom
> within the reach of the nuclear physicist.[1]

Galileo founded the principles of the experimental
scientific method, but it was Sir Isaac Newton (1642-
1726), who is generally credited with the most successful, if not the first, thorough use of mathematical
modeling to explain and predict physical phenomena.
One of Newton's greatest scientific achievements, and
certainly his most important from the modern OR viewpoint, was his ability to have taken the observations
of Tycho Brahe and the empirical principles of Johannes
Kepler in all their bewildering complexity, and to
develop from them an elegant, accurate and simple

---

1 Herbert A. Simon and Allen Newell, "Heuristic Problem
Solving: The Next Advance in Operations Research," Opns.
Res., 6 (January - February, 1958), 6.

mathematical model of gravitational force in the solar
system based on the representation of all of its bodies
as point masses. In addition, it was Newton's ability
to generalize the use of mathematical models and their
extensions to other areas, that distinguished him as
one of the greatest mathematicians and scientists of
all time, and only parenthetically as an early contributor to OR.

> Newton's theory of universal gravitation
> explained first of all the notion of apples
> which he saw falling from a tree in the orchard
> of Woolsthorpe. Had this been its full range
> of extension, the theory would only rank with
> other minor hypotheses which populate fields
> that have not yet become completely scientific.[1]

Much of the scientific work of the nineteenth
century also had the seeds of modern OR investigations.[2]
In 1859, Charles Darwin (1809-1882), published his
Origin of Species which can be classified as an early
OR study (without detracting from its immense scientific
impact), based on the fact that it resulted from more
than twenty years of long painstaking research on living
and fossil species. The lengthy datawere carefully
worked into a large system model, in what can be considered as an OR global optimization, without having had to
resort to quantitative mathematical methods.

---

1 Margenau, 141.

2 Philip M. Morse, "Operations Research - An Application
of Scientific Method," The Technology Review, 55 (May,
1953), 3.

In 1865, Gregor J. Mendel (1822-1884), also after long and careful observation, formulated a statistical model for the reproduction of the pea plant. The simple model Mendel devised to predict the complex behavior of genetic heredity would raise the envy of any modern OR analyst. The model was a controlled compromise, between the attempt to understand the chemical behavior of genes and to explain the actual outcomes of their interbreeding.

In 1868, Dmitri I. Mendelyeev (1834-1907), after classifying the properties of the sixty odd elements known at that time, observed that they could be conveniently grouped into families based on their atomic weights and valences. The model he devised, now called the Periodic Table, was simple and elegant, yet powerful enough to successfully predict the existence, and the properties of elements not yet discovered-- a worthy goal for any OR model formulation.

The Formulators of Operations Research

Although the previously cited individuals could all be classified as among the early contributors to modern OR, their studies all lacked the total set of ingredients which can be used to unmistakably identify an OR study in the modern sense. These essential ingredients may be summarized as the "10Ms": the manipulation of mathematical models to measure the management of men, machines, methods, and money in their milieu.

Charles Babbage (1792-1871), probably was the
first person to have satisfied this 10M criterion.
In 1834 he translated his mathematical models to a
working "difference engine" that was designed to
fulfill his lifelong ambition of eliminating human
and mechanical "... errors in astronomical and
mathematical tables, by having machines not only
calculate them but print them directly without human
intervention."[1] Babbage's goal of inventing an
automatic calculator in order to eliminate human
clerical activity and therefore human error, was
inspired by M. de Prony's mass production of logarithm
tables, de Prony himself having been motivated by
Adam Smith's treatment of the division of labor in
pin manufacture.[2]

Although no one person is associated with the
entire development of digital computers (which play
so prominent a role in modern OR simulation studies),
the name of Charles Babbage is most often associated
with the creation of their mechanical predecessors,
and the formulation of "... the critically important
idea of a conditional transfer operation."[3] His

---

1 Trevor I. Williams, ed., A Bibliographical Dictionary of Scientists (New York: Wiley - Interscience,
1969), 24.

2 Simon and Newell, 1-3.

3 Ibid., 3.

overall contribution to modern OR was demonstrated
by the fact that:

> Perhaps more than any man since Leonardo
> da Vinci he exemplified in his life and work
> the powerful ways in which fundamental science
> could contribute to practical affairs, and
> practical affairs to science.[1]

Babbage's one unrealistic position, by modern OR
standards, was his negative decision to eliminate human
activity as a means of dealing with the inherent
uncertainties involved in the studies of how men,
machines, and methods interact. However, this hardly
diminished the magnitude of his achievements in the
realm of computer developments.

The application of OR type procedures to business
activities had its roots in the late nineteenth, and
the early twentieth centuries. Frederick W. Taylor
(1856-1915), played a principal role in this transfer,
since he perfected time and motion studies, "... converted industrial engineering into a profession and can,
with some justification, be considered the father of
Scientific Management."[2]

After working his way up from steelworker to gang
boss, and finally to chief engineer in 1899, he began

---

1 Simon and Newell, 1-2.

2 Richard I. Levin and C. A. Kirkpatrick, Quantitative
Approaches to Management (New York: McGraw-Hill Book Co.,
1965), 6.

his noted career as an efficiency expert by successfully reorganizing manufacturing plant operations,
shop accounting practices, and sales department activities for the Bethlehem Steel Company. Later he
prescribed a step by step method of improving brick-
laying methods after a painstakingly careful study.[1]
However, it was Taylor's legendary work on the shovel
problem that most closely resembled a modern OR study.[2]

"Management had always assumed that the largest
shovel a man could fill and carry was the size to
maximize output."[3] Taylor doubted this premise, and
set out to test its validity through direct experimentation. Here then was a classical trade-off problem
with an objective function that had to be maximized.
If the shovel load was too heavy, the worker tired
too quickly, and output dropped off. The solution was
to find the optimal shovel load that could be handled
in a work day by a "first-class worker" (Taylor
preferred to base models on the ideal rather than the
average worker), so as to yield the greatest moved

---

1 David W. Miller and Martin K. Starr, Executive
Decisions and Operations Research (2nd ed.; Englewood
Cliffs, N. J.: Prentice-Hall, 1969), 65.
2 J. W. Pocock, "Operations Research and the
Management Consultant," Opns. Res., 1 (May, 1953), 137.
3 Levin and Kirkpatrick, 6-7.

tonnage with the least fatigue. Taylor's studies led
him to conclude that shovels should be designed to hold
about twenty-one pounds of load, regardless of material
density, in order to obtain optimal output.[1]

During Taylor's day it was not uncommon to base
managerial decisions on past practice or intuitive
insight. Taylor's basic contribution to OR studies in
business and industry was to demonstrate the inappro-
priateness of such procedures, and the need for the careful collection, the classification, and the analysis of
data through experimentation, so as to formulate laws
and principles of operations that were more reliable
than they were arbitrary.

Taylor himself observed that his work did not
entail a new discovery or invention but merely represented a new way of combining data.[2] By modern OR
standards Taylor's primary concern with the efficient
operations of men and machines is now viewed as a
secondary consideration since efficiency should follow
logically from careful planning. Yet it has been noted
that "Taylor's ideas on operational research had the
essence of our [OR] profession, but the fire was not

---

1 Pocock, 137.
2 Frederick W. Taylor, "Principles of Scientific Management," in Scientific Management (3rd ed.; New York:
Harper and Brothers, 1947), 139-140.

kindled by the spark."[1]

A. K. Erlang (1878-1928), joined the Copenhagen Telephone Company in 1908, and he worked there the rest of his life. Since the company already "... had the distinction of endorsing and supporting several <u>important</u> investigations in probability theory,"[2] related to telephone networks, it provided an ideal environment for Erlang to establish the foundations of the modern OR theory of queueing which is sometimes more descriptively referred to as waiting-line or bottle-neck theory. Erlang's research was motivated by the then startling discovery that the Gestalt effects of a working automatic telephone exchange were not the same as the summed effects of its individual component relays. This was one of the first observations on the potential dangers of suboptimization.

Erlang was thus faced with the problem of establishing a controlled compromise to balance engineering and OR considerations. The former involved the best means of installing complicated automatic switching circuits.

---

1 Ellis A. Johnson, "The Long-Range Future of Operational Research," <u>Opns. Res.</u>, 8 (January-February, 1960), 3.

2 Byron O. Marshall, Jr., "Queueing Theory," in <u>Operations Research for Management</u> Vol. I, ed. by Joseph F. McCloskey and Florence N. Trefethen (Baltimore: The Johns Hopkins Press, 1966), 134.

The latter was concerned with predicting the optimal
level between too few circuits with their resultant
long-time delays at peak demand periods, and too many
circuits with their associated high fixed-dollar costs.
To solve the problem he developed one of the first OR
models built around strictly mathematical formulations.
The solution to the mathematical model Erlang had
created proved to be prohibitive before he was able
to establish that telephone calls arriving at the
exchange could be approximated by a Poisson distribution, and that telephone service times followed an
essentially exponential distribution. Erlang's only
shortcoming as a modern OR analyst involved the
relatively trivial point that he was unable or
reluctant to extend his queueing results for telephone
networks to similar problems in other areas.

Erlang's style of attacking problems was Socratic
in nature, very much in the manner of modern OR consultants. He was reluctant to provide direct answers to
posed questions, preferring instead to engage in
lengthy discussions designed to elucidate all aspects
of the subject so that the inquirer might solve the
problem independently,[1] and perhaps so that Erlang

1 Thomas L. Saaty, Mathematical Models of Operations
Research (New York: McGraw-Hill Book Co., 1959), 6.

himself might have time to set up a solution. His
most important work, <u>Solution of Some Problems in the
Theory of Probabilities of Significance in Automatic
Telephone Exchanges</u> was published in 1917. It
contained formulas for measuring power loss and for
predicting waiting times in telephone networks. Based
on "... the principle of statistical equilibrium;
these now well-known formulas are of fundamental
importance to the theory of telephone traffic,"[1] and
anticipated by forty years the concepts of modern
queueing theory.

Thomas Alva Edison (1847-1931), was a scientist
of unsurpassed inventiveness and energy, who acquired
more than three hundred patents in his lifetime. At
Menlo Park he developed "... the first 'invention-
factory', the forerunner of the vast research organizations of modern industry,"[2] such as Bell Laboratories.
He and his staff worked on as many as fifty inventions
simultaneously. Edison did not hesitate to work up to
twenty hours a day to patiently and exhaustively test
thousands of alternative solutions, as he did in finding

1 E. Brockmeyer,   H. L. Halstrom, and
Arne Jensen, "The Life and Works of A. K. Erlang,"
<u>Transactions of the Danish Academy of Technical Sciences</u>
<u>2 (1948), 17.</u>
2 Trevor Williams, 159.

the cotton-carbon filament for his first electric
light bulb. In order to properly plan for the
electrical needs of the first central power station
at Pearl Street in New York City, Edison conducted
what is regarded as the first market survey on record
by carefully noting all the gas lights in the area and
the length of time they were burned.[1]

Edison's mechanical and inventive talents have
never been surpassed. However, the work which by its
nature, format and style can be used to classify him
as an early OR contributor was that done for the
United States Naval Research Laboratory, whose creation he had advocated as early as 1910. His pleas
were finally heeded when Secretary of the Navy Daniels
asked Edison on July 7, 1915 to head the Laboratory
since it had become apparent that the Navy urgently
needed the "... machinery and facilities for utilizing
the natural inventive genius of Americans to meet new
conditions of warfare..."[2] Although Edison was tapped
for his inventive genius rather than his executive
abilities, he quickly demonstrated his versatility by

1 Norman R. Speiden, "Thomas A. Edison: Sketch of
Activities, 1874-1881," Science, 105 (February 7, 1947),
140.

2 A. Hoyt Taylor, "Thomas A. Edison and the Naval
Research Laboratory," Science, 105 (February 7, 1947),
148.

the clever identification and analysis of problems that would have been the envy of any modern OR analyst.

In cooperation with the British Admiralty, he undertook a study to improve allied activities against the new tactics of submarine warfare perfected by the Germans. He was charged with devising methods of increasing submarine kills. However, after briefly experimenting with listening devices, he correctly concluded that his first priority should be involved with the saving of ships rather than with the killing of submarines. "This choice of the correct measure of effectiveness led him into an operations research activity."[1]

In order to prepare appropriate recommendations, Edison made a thorough, one year statistical study of all shipping to and from British and French ports. Thus, OR began in the U. S. Navy during World War I, and not, as widely held, with the antisubmarine problems of World War II. Tragically however, his data and results were needlessly duplicated by the allies during World War II because they had been unappreciatively filed away by the British Admiralty without ever having been implemented.

Another of Edison's major accomplishments in his

---

1 William F. Whitmore, "Edison and Operations Research," Opns. Res., 1 (February, 1953), 83.

World War I OR studies dealt with refuting the widely
held belief that the tactic of zigzagging for a
merchant ship traveling less than ten knots per hour
was an effective means of avoiding torpedoes. Edison
achieved this result by devising a mechanical simulation device that "... foreshadowed the use of a
tactical game board, together with some empirical
notions of sweep widths,"[1] that are so crucial to
modern OR search theory and war gaming.

Judging from the fact that his OR studies were
buried in British Admiralty files and forgotten by
the United States Navy, Edison was either too far
ahead of his time or he was the victim of a common
OR malady -- the failure of an analyst to properly
communicate or implement the results of an OR study.
Edison's only shortcoming by modern OR standards
(but which may have been one of his greatest inventive
assets), was his failure to set a proper balance
between theory and experiment which resulted in his
virtual dependence on inefficient trial and error
methods, and his actual disdain for mathematical
modeling.

Frederick William Lanchester (1868-1946), was an
inventor as well as a theoretician. His inventions of

---

1 Whitmore, 83.

a perfectly balanced, almost silent engine, a noise-
less rear axle, a direct-drive fast gear, a superior
spring suspension, a self-correcting steering
mechanism, and a low-tension magneto ignition system
made possible the development of the modern automobile.
His theoretical explanations of the aerodynamics of
airfoils, and the effectiveness of the cambered wing,
anticipated modern aircraft design.[1] Lanchester made
some of the first applications of mathematics to the
analysis of combat situations during World War I,
and foresaw the use of aircraft in warfare.[2]

Lanchester analyzed the effects of military
combat in terms of two variables, the force of the
unit (f) and the size of the unit (N), and developed
his now famous n-square law for a stand-off between
two opposing forces: $f_1 N_1^2 = f_2 N_2^2$. For example,
using Lanchester's n-square law, a police detachment
outnumbered ten to one would have to be able to
deliver a force one hundred times greater than a
rioting mob in order to hold it at bay. Actually,
the n-square law has been fitted accurately to only

1 Joseph F. McCloskey, "Of Horseless Carriages, Flying
Machines and Operations Research," Opns. Res., 4
(April, 1956), 143-144.

2 Clayton J. Thomas, "Military Gaming," in Progress
in Operations Research, Vol. I, Russell L. Ackoff, ed.
(New York: John Wiley & Sons, Inc., 1966), 450.

several isolated military engagements, nevertheless,
it has been successfully used in modern military
gaming, political campaigning, advertising promotions,
and industrial competition. Lanchester analyzed the
British success in the Battle of Trafalgar of 1805,
and observed that the British Admiral Horatio
"... Nelson, if not actually acquainted with the
n-square law, must have had some equivalent basis on
which to figure his tactical values."[1]

Lanchester recognized "... the power of scientific insight and mathematical tools in the solution of
operational problems long before the term 'operations
research' was coined."[2] Unfortunately, Lanchester's
works were not fully appreciated or understood until
years after he had proposed them. Lanchester himself
commented in 1916 that "there are many who will be
inclined to cavil at any mathematial or semi-mathemati-
cal treatment of [military conflicts]..."[3] due to the
fact that too many unknowns are involved in the analysis.
It has been claimed that due to Lanchester's retirement,
and the cloak of secrecy surrounding OR during World War

1 Frederick W. Lanchester, "Mathematics in Warfare,"
in The World of Mathematics, Vol. 4, notes and comments
by James R. Newman (New York: Simon and Schuster), 2157.

2 McCloskey, 141.

3 Lanchester, 2143-2144.

II, that he may never have realized before his death
that he had probably pioneered yet another discipline
-- OR.[1] Though Lanchester never achieved the
distinction he deserved for his contributions to OR,
it is a fitting tribute that the highest OR honor
the Operations Research Society of America bestows
annually is called the Lanchester Prize, and is
awarded for the best written exposition dealing with
OR.

In the early twentieth century it became the
practice of many companies in highly competitive
fields to hire consultants in the hope that they
would be able to improve company operations. Due
to the nature of the consulting work, it was
necessary to keep most of the study results secret,
and consequently reports of management consultant
activities were seldom published. One of the first
and most successful of these consultants, whose
methods anticipated modern OR analyses in the retail
sales area, was Horace C. Levinson (1895-   ). His
work provided "... the best pre-World War II example
of a natural scientist who applied his analytic
abilities to problems of management."[2]

---

1   McCloskey, 145.
2   Levin and Kirkpatrick, 8.

In 1924 Levinson became associated with a small
mail-order house. The major problem he tackled and
solved for the company was the optimal way to deal
with the problem that "... just over 30 per cent of
the dollar volume of its gross sales represented
returned goods."[1] After an exhaustive study, he
found that the proper way of dealing with unwanted
goods was to concentrate the company's efforts on
reducing unclaimed postal returns rather than attempt-
ing to reduce dissatisfied customer returns. Levinson's
analysis resulted in the mail-order operation rule of thumb
that orders should be shipped within five days of
receipt in order to reduce unclaimed postal returns
to a minimum.[2]

Based on "his success in predicting general human
reactions from the collection and analysis of great
quantities of data,..."[3] L. Bamberger and Company
asked Levinson, in 1938, to examine the effect of net
sales, on what was then an innovation, of remaining
open to 9:00 P.M. on Wednesdays. Levinson considered
every measurable variable including employee prefer-

---

1 Horace C. Levinson, "Experiences in Commercial
Operations Research," in McCloskey and Trefethen, 268.
2 Levinson, 270.
3 Saaty, 7.

ences, and he concluded that despite some transfer
of sales to Wednesday from other days, the practice
of late openings increased total sales by 1.3 per
cent of weekly sales.[1]

Levinson's basic approach to the use of OR in
business involved solving

> ... those fragments of a total problem that
> [were] amenable to quantitative formulation.
> The suboptimized solutions [could] then be
> considered by top management together with
> the intangibles, the unquantifiable elements
> of the problem.[2]

Levinson thus extended the OR sphere to the business
community, and refined OR modeling by introducing
higher mathematics into its formulation and solution.[3]
He was so successful that in 1949 the U. S. National
Research Council appointed Levinson Chairman of a
committee charged with fostering interest in, and
disseminating information about, the non-military
uses of OR.

Economics was the first non-physical science
to make extensive use of OR models in order to explain
economic theories. Since the works of the economist
Francois Quesnay (1694-1774), there has been a close
interchange between the developments of econometrics

---

1 Levinson, 276.
2 Ibid., 265.
3 Saaty, 7.

and mathematical modeling. T. M. Whitin,[1] made an excellent case for the role that economics has played in initiating investigations that require the use of global and suboptimum methods of OR.

Whitin singled out Erich Schneider (1900-   ), as having anticipated, by almost twenty years, the application of linear programming techniques to production scheduling problems. Schneider was also credited with having anticipated quadratic programming by "... introducing a quadratic, cost function to be minimized subject to inequalities imposed by the conditions that capacity [could] not be exceeded and sales [had to] be fulfilled."[2] His major OR contribution was his ability to identify all the key variables of a problem, work them into an interrelated mathematical model, and then derive an optimal solution. Schneider's original analysis,[3] dealt with a discrete rather than a continuous time domain, but this shortcoming is modified in current OR practice by using sufficiently small discrete time intervals to theoretically approximate the continuous analysis.

---

1 T. M. Whitin, "Erich Schneider's Inventory Control Analysis," Opns. Res., 2 (August, 1954), 329-334.

2 Whitin, 332.

3 Erich Schneider, "Absatz, Produktion und Lagerhaltung bei ein facher Produktion," Arch. Math. Wirstshafts v. Sozialforschung, Band IV, Heft I, Leipzig (1938), 99-120.

The Historical Emergence of Modern Operations Research

Until the late 1800s most industrial organizations
were owned and managed by the same individual, "...
employed only a handful of people, and occupied a space
about the size of a two-car garage."[1] Even with the
advent of the industrial revolution the rate of growth
of most companies was such that the executives could
keep abreast of new developments. Consequently,
most industries could be effectively managed by slight
modifications of past practice. It was not until the
1920s, as competition became intense and profits more
difficult to obtain, that some executives sought
outside help in running their companies. Due to the
highly secret nature of such consultation, researchers
were often forbidden from publishing their findings.
Perhaps the best known case is that of the developer
of the student t-distribution, W. S. Gosset who wrote
under the pen name of "Student" to prevent discovery
by his employer, an Irish brewery.

"The genesis of management consulting is somewhat
obscured in the mists of time."[2] However, its written
history, as previously noted, began around 1885 with

---

1 Russell L. Ackoff and Patrick Rivett, A Manager's
Guide to Operations Research (New York: John Wiley
& Sons, Inc., 1967), 1.
2 Pocock, 137.

the investigations of men such as Taylor and
Henry L. Gantt. The motivating force behind the
development in 1929, of the Association of Management
Engineers, which included some thirty-nine established
management consulting firms of the time, was the
increased application of science to business, industry
and commerce.[1]

Several factors probably prevented the rapidly
expanding field of management consulting from developing naturally into the modern OR discipline. "One
great trouble... was that a great army of cranks and
charlatans [emerged] who wished to make money out of
the new scientific management enthusiasm."[2] Secondly,
the craze to obtain precise measurements in time and
motion studies as applied to labor and products in the
1920s was carried "... to such a point that the human
values inherent in a production operation became
somewhat lost."[3] Finally, with the advent of mass
production assembly lines, and the impact of the
depression there was less contact between executives
and consultants, and thus fewer opportunities to

---

1   Pocock, 138.
2   Robert F. Rinehart, "Threats to the Growth of
Operations Research in Business and Industry," Opns.
Res., 2 (August, 1954), 231, quoting from a 1911 letter
written by Frederick W. Taylor.
3   Pocock, 138.

demonstrate the capabilities of OR type studies.[1]

During the time up to 1938 an entirely new technology and strategy for waging war had been emerging. Military leaders, whose experience in such matters was discontinuous due to the two decades between wars, were suddenly confronted with the necessity of waging war with equipment, and within systems, for which they had hardly any actual, first-hand experience. With the pressures of World War II imminent, and the first significant call to put their research talents to profitable use since pre-depression days, it was not surprising that "some scientists put aside their prejudices against applied research and took up the challenge."[2]

Charles P. Snow has noted that, "in the 1914-18 war, A. V. Hill's scientists were testing antiaircraft gunnery and were carrying out what we should later have called operational research."[3] However, it was not until the advent of World War II, that OR blossomed into a scientific discipline in its own right. There is the oversimplified view that, "operational research

---

1 Ackoff and Rivett, 5.

2 Ibid.

3 Charles P. Snow, Science and Government (Cambridge, Mass.: Harvard University Press, 1961), 86.

was really born out of the 'Battle of Britain',"[1] but a more accurate view would be that, "operations research began as an organized form of research just before the outbreak of World War II."[2]

The first study labeled as OR, began at Bawsdey in the United Kingdom during 1937. It centered around the optimal use and positioning of the newly discovered radiolocation method (now called radar), in order to detect enemy aerial attacks more quickly. The investigators sought and found answers to problems such as:

1. how to offset possible enemy jamming of the equipment,
2. how to couple the new system with the older system of human sighting, identification, and reporting of planes, and
3. how to discover and correct flaws in the aerial defense systems.

This early success of an OR labeled activity involved the cooperative efforts of R. G. Hart, H. Larnder, G. A. Roberts, A. P. Rowe, J. G. Todd, E. C. Williams, J. Woodford, and Robert Watson-Watt who was generally recognized as the chief developer of RADAR technology.[3] The Bawdsey section was soon

---

1 Goodeve, 377.

2 Florence N. Trefethen, "A History of Operations Research," in McCloskey and Trefethen, 3.

3 J. G. Crowther and R. Whiddington, Science at War (New York: Philosophical Library, 1948), 2.

transferred to the R.A.F. Figher Command at Stanmore, and "... it steadily extended its scope of activities beyond radar and its uses and, by the time of the Battle of Britain, was consulted on an ever-widening variety of subjects..."[1] Similar sections were soon set up by the British Navy to study antisubmarine problems, and by the British Army to study anti-aircraft and radar problems.[2]

Eric C. Williams, who was a Junior Scientific Officer at the Bawdsey Research Station, pointed out that the military research done there did not repre-sent a sudden debut for OR. However, the newness that analysts did bring to such OR studies, was a faster, more systematic means of evaluating military methods and weaponry. The leisurely days which allowed events and processes to work themselves out naturally were gone. It was clear that the trial and error procedures of yesterday would, if not streamlined, turn out to be the trial and catastrophe events of modern warfare.[3]

The desperate emergency which engulfed Great Britain's military in the early days of World War II

---

1 Crowther and Whiddington, 93.

2 Omond Solandt, "Observation, Experiment, and Measure-ment in Operations Research," Opns. Res., 3 (February, 1955), 1-2.

3 Eric Williams, "Reflections on Operations Research," Opns. Res., 2 (November, 1954), 441.

was the catalyst for the accelerated growth of
modern OR. The first systematic and complete application of the scientific method to real-life situations
was created by the pressing problems of military
logistics, strategy, and tactics. Men from a variety
of backgrounds and disciplines were forged into teams
to grapple with large-scale problems in the hope that
the combined cooperative perspective of their diverse
disciplines would simplify some of the overwhelmingly
complicated situations.

> In a sense by chance, they demonstrated,
> where given the opportunity to, that a great
> storehouse of human knowledge could be used
> successfully in situations that previously
> had been considered too chaotic, too random,
> too complex, or too uncertain for any other
> treatment than unaided intuition and
> judgement...

> Viewed in this manner, we observe in
> operations research not a novel, startling,
> and unproven technology, but rather the
> evolution of well-known thought processes
> into broader and perhaps more complex fields.[1]

British Army officers had observed that the
battle location performance of the new antiaircraft
gunsights coupled with radar to provide slant range,
bearing and elevation of attacking enemy bombers
was in marked discrepancy with the manufacturer's
test performance data. In August, 1940, P. M. S.
Blackett was asked to investigate this problem, and

1 M. L. Hurni, "Observations on Operations Research,"
Opns. Res., 2 (August, 1954), 236.

he decided that the discrepancy in performance
required, on the site, scientific observations, during
the actual operation of the radar gunsights.[1] In
order to make these on the site observations, Blackett
formed an interdisciplinary study team (which was later
to become known as "Blackett's Circus"), composed
and selected in the following order: two physiologists,
two mathematical physicists, an astrophysicist, an
Army officer, an ex-surveyor, and a third
physiologist.[2]

In a single stroke of insight Blackett had
established the interdisciplinary team approach to
modern OR problems, but as is unfortunately the case
with many important innovations, the discoverer left
no clues as to the reasons for making such a decision.
Morse, who cooperated with Blackett later, speculated
that since Blackett was an outstanding physicist he
would be able to uncover any technical flaws in the
equipment itself. Consequently, he selected two
physiologists first so that they could uncover any
human measurement errors that were present during the
actual operations. Undoubtedly, the sighting experiences of the other OR team members would also be used

---

1 Trefethen, 6.
2 Crowther and Whiddington, 96.

to this end.[1]

Blackett's Circus quickly solved the radar gunsight problem, which turned out to be caused by a combination of human and equipment errors. They were likely the first OR group "... to demonstrate the value of the mixed-team approach to operational problems."[2] It should be noted that this first Blackett team had established its authority and title as the "... Anti-Aircraft Command Research Group by making a rubber stamp with the initials A. A. C. R. G. It is not known whether any more formal authorization or recognition was ever obtained."[3]

The news of OR work probably first came to the United States of America after James B. Conant, then Chairman of the National Defense Research Committee, visited England in the autumn of 1940.[4] By May, 1942, the U. S. Navy, interested in antisubmarine studies, helped to establish an OR team headed by Morse. The unit which included George Kimball, Robert Rinehart, and Bill Shockley decided to improve operations against German U-boats by first analyzing

1 Personal interview with Philip M. Morse, Ph.D., Director of the Operations Research Center, and Professor of Physics, Massachusetts Institute of Technology, at Cambridge, Mass., August 17, 1970.

2 Trefethen, 6.

3 Crowther and Whiddington, 96.

4 Trefethen, 12.

the results of attacks by U. S. planes and ships
against enemy submarines sighted in U. S. coastal
waters.

The Morse team also encountered an initial
discrepancy. The reports of the search pilots did
not correlate with the naval reports of submarine
sightings when computed speeds and directions were
established. After insisting on and seeing the
search methods first hand despite strong naval
objections, the OR team discovered that the pilots
were filling out the detailed reports arbitrarily
because no one had bothered to explain the significance of such reports to them. The accuracy of the
submarine location data improved markedly after the
pilots were properly briefed.[1]

Many other OR units were set up on both sides
of the Atlantic during World War II by all branches
of the Allied military. Their successes varied
from minor OR breakthroughs to major OR achievements.[2]
It was during this time that OR analysts took the
giant step of considering operational problems worthy
of consideration as formal research problems. It is

1 Morse, Personal Interview.

2 Consult, Crowther and Whiddington, and Trefethen
for more detailed histories of OR activities during
World War II.

perfectly clear that the methods of modern OR studies

fully emerged during World War II, and that:

> The consideration of a problem in
> terms of its relationships to an entire
> operation, making necessary the study of
> additional, operationally-related problems,
> was probably the one achievement which most
> clearly distinguished World War II opera-
> tional problems from earlier research activities.[1]

---

[1] Trefethen, 11.

CHAPTER III

THE PHILOSOPHY OF OPERATIONS RESEARCH

The philosophical foundations of OR are still
in their formative stages, and are evolving gradually
from the studies and experiences of OR practitioners.
In its own right,

> operational research may be regarded as a
> branch of philosophy, as an attitude of mind
> towards the relation between man and environ-
> ment; and as a body of methods for the solution
> of problems which arise in that relationship.[1]

Regardless of the various views on the nature of OR,
there is general agreement on guidelines for the
procedural order needed to conduct OR studies of
systems. However, the literature does not contain
a complete listing in any one source, so that the
following ten steps, recommended for the OR study of
systems, were obtained after an extensive synthesis.[2]

1. The observations and study of the system's

    functions and operations.

2. The determination, definition, and delimitation

    of the system's problems.

---

1 M. G. Kendall, "The Teaching of Operational Research,"
Operational Research Quarterly, 9 (December, 1958), 267.

2 For example, a brief version of seven of these steps
is found in Patrick Rivett, An Introduction to Operations
Research (New York: Basic Books, Inc., 1968), 12.

3. The selection of the system's variables that
    are to be controlled, measured, and traded-off.

4. The establishment of measurement criteria,
    and subjective considerations of the system's
    variables, and uncertainties.

5. The collection and analysis of the system's data.

6. The search for appropriate model representations
    of the system.

7. The manipulation of the model representations so
    as to obtain optimum system trade-offs.

8. The examination of the accuracy, and the
    practicality of the system optimums derived
    from the models.

9. The communication and implementation of the model
    optimums into the system.

10. The reevaluation and adjustment of the implemented
    optimums through regular system monitoring and
    feedback analysis.

The observation and study of the system's functions and operations

In certain studies indirect observation is necessary and/or unavoidable. Thus, in nuclear physics,
subatomic particles are studied by path traces left
in cloud chambers. In forensic science, identification
clues are studied through evidence traces left at the
scene of an investigation. Nevertheless, it is still

advisable for OR studies to obtain as much first
hand knowledge and familiarity with the equipment,
the methods, and the operations of the system under
study as possible.

First hand observation is particularly essential
to OR studies because experience has indicated that
many important facts concerning system operations
"... can often only be determined by having a
technically trained observer question the operational
personnel first hand."[1] This is often due to the
fact that management's initial statement to the
investigating OR team about the nature of a system's
problem "... is more apt to be a revelation of
symptoms than a diagnosis."[2]

On the now classical OR analyses of problems in
submarine warfare, solved by Morse and others during
World War II,[3] Stafford Beer observed that before the
OR team arrived, the Navy viewed these problems as
abstractions on a blackboard, rather than derivations
from real-life operations.[4] In fact, when Morse

1 Philip M. Morse and George E. Kimball, Methods of
Operations Research (1st ed. rev.; Cambridge, Mass.:
The M. I. T. Press, 1970), 8.

2 C. West Churchman, Russell L. Ackoff, and E. Leonard
Arnoff, Introduction to Operations Research (New York:
John Wiley & Sons, Inc., 1961), 68.

3 Consult, Morse and Kimball, 38-60, for more details.

4 Stafford Beer, Decision and Control, (London:
John Wiley, 1966), 48.

requested that members of his team accompany the
patrol planes in their search for German U-boats,
the commanding officer retorted "Why do you have
to do that? We've got experts who can tell you
all you want to know!"[1] Such responses from
managers in areas such as industry, business, and
criminal justice (CJ) are too often the reality
rather than the exception.

The typical OR study does not lend itself
to laboratory experimentation. Thus, the OR analyst
must invariably observe the real-life situation first
hand, in all its nuances, in order to observe subtle
system interactions, previously overlooked factors,
gather first hand information, delimit the problem,
and understand the effects of the personnel upon
system operations.

The determination, definition, and delimitation of the system's problems

The formulation of the problem is probably the
most important part of any study. There is an old
adage that a problem well put is half solved. In
many cases however, how to put a problem well is

1 Personal interview with Philip M. Morse, Ph.D.,
Director of the Operations Research Center, and
Professor of Physics, Massachusetts Institute of
Technology, Cambridge, Mass., August 17, 1970.

neither simple nor obvious. More frequently it is
the true nature of a system's problem that remains
hidden, even though a wealth of potential solutions
can be formulated. If the management of a system
cannot recognize that they have a problem, then, to
paraphrase the psychologists' credo, OR analysts
can hardly be expected to provide meaningful
suggestions and feasible solutions.

One of the basic tasks of the OR analyst is
to take ill-defined problems, and translate them into
a formulation amenable to study. This is no mean task,
and deservedly, "many scientists owe their greatness
not to their skill in solving problems but to their
wisdom in choosing them."[1]

The eventual success of an OR study depends on
an appropriately accurate formulation of the problem.

> Formulating the problem is usually a
> sequential process. An initial formulation
> is completed and research proceeds, but in
> proceeding the problem is subjected to almost
> continuous and progressive reformulation and
> refinement.[2]

An illustration of this principle occurred in the
analysis of why a U. S. Air Force bomber squadron

---

1 Charles Hitch, "Uncertainties in Operations
Research," Opns. Res., 8 (July - August, 1960), 439,
who credits the quote to E. Bright Wilson.
2 Churchman, et al., 105.

stationed on a Pacific island in 1944 was being
fired on when leaving and returning to base, more
than any other squadron in the area, by U. S. Navy
vessels stationed nearby. The OR analyst assigned
to resolve the problem initially traced the complex
electronic circuits of the "Interrogate -- Friend
or Foe" (IFF) equipment, and made statistical
calculations of the incidents; all to no avail.
After a week of such analyses, he discovered that
the resolution of the problem merely required a
reminder to the pilots to turn on their IFF units
when they took off.[1]

The availability of an OR technique and
concomitantly a readily available solution should not
dictate the statement of a problem in terms which are
not compatible with the realities of the system.
However tempting such an approach might be, it is
bound to produce invalid results since, "the wrong
problem is a problem that is not a real problem,
although it often has a precise, mathematical solution."[2]

---

1 Dean E. Wooldridge, "Operations Research -- The
Scientists' Invasion of the Business World,"
The Journal of Industrial Engineering, VII (September-
October, 1956), 230.

2 Thomas M. Ware, "An Executive's Viewpoint,"
Opns. Res., 7 (January-February, 1959), 7.

The selection of the system's variables that are to be controlled, measured, and traded-off

The current emphasis on the environmental sciences has demonstrated the overriding point that all aspects of a system are interrelated. Thus, OR studies must be wary of over-simplified investigations and should be prepared to "... trace relationships a long way back--and forward, and sideways."[1]

That OR studies usually involve consideration of many variables is generally accepted. But then all real problems involve a large number of variables, the difficulty lies in the selection of those variables that can be neglected so that the preliminary analysis can begin. As a rough idea of just how many variables must be contended with typically by various disciplines, consider the following sketch.[2]

Number of Independent Variables

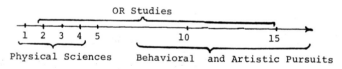

---

1 Beer, 245.

2 Adapted from W. C. Randels, "Some Qualities to be Desired in Operations Research Personnel," Opns. Res., 4 (February, 1956), 117.

A formidable difficulty exists in first sorting the variables into those that can be reasonably controlled and measured. Those system variables that can be controlled and measured, must then be assigned according to the priorities which conform to the formulation of the problem, the objectives of the study, and the values of the operators and managers of the system.

Invariably this trade-off procedure amounts to finding an optimal ordering between two or more competing variables. The method of doing this involves suboptimization whereby the OR analyst must reduce the problem to one of workable size, while simultaneously keeping the overall system's objectives in prominent view, so as not to be led into the potential dangers of suboptimization.

The establishment of measurement criteria, and subjective considerations of the system's variables and uncertainties

Unavoidably coupled to the selection of variables and objectives, is the problem of establishing appropriate cirteria and subjective considerations for the measurement of these variables and objectives along with their associated degrees of uncertainty. Assume that as an example, the objective is to improve the effectiveness of police patrol activity in deterring crime. Some possible variables would be, methods of police deployment, crime incidence, apprehension rates, and the crime deterrence rate.

A logical question would arise over which criterion to select in order to measure change in the effectiveness of police patrol activity.[1] Should it be the number of reported crimes, the average police response time, the number of arrests, the patrol density at each location, or the number of deterred crimes. Actually, it is the last criterion that is most crucial in this case, but as is often true, this is a criterion that is most difficult to measure with any specified degree of certainty. Typically, the OR analyst has no alternative but to select one of the other criteria based simply on the fact that it is more amenable to measurement, even though it may be less sensitive and not as pertinent to the system's objectives.

This pragmatic selection of measurement criteria can easily misdirect an OR study, because "very often failure to choose the proper measures of effectiveness can lead to completely wrong conclusions about the problem."[2] Nevertheless, if the OR study is to proceed,

---

1 Consult, David G. Olson, "A Preventive Patrol Model" (paper presented at the 36th national meeting of the Operations Research Society of America, Miami Beach, Florida, November 11, 1969).

2 Thomas L. Saaty, Mathematical Methods of Operations Research, (New York: McGraw-Hill Book Co., 1959), 29.

the analyst must select those measurement criteria
that are closest to the system's objectives and
quantifiable enough to be modeled.

The selection of appropriate and accurate
measurement criteria is therefore studded with
uncertainties. As Charles Hitch has indicated, the
operations researcher ignores these uncertainties
at his own peril.[1] In OR studies, "uncertainty must
be accepted; it is there; it is ineluctable."[2]

The uncertainties that do arise in OR system
studies may vary from the obvious to the more subtle
ones such as the Heisenberg uncertainty principle in
physics. Simply stated, this means that it is
impossible to know simultaneously both the position
and the momentum of an electron. It is not certain
whether this phenomenon is due to observational
difficulties, or if it is an inherent property of
nature. Phrased somewhat differently, the OR analyst
must be aware that in establishing measurement
criteria it may very well be that the subjectivity
of the system objectives and the values of the OR
methodology used in seeking optimum solutions are not
simultaneously knowable or compatible.

---

1 Charles Hitch, "Uncertainties in Operations
Research," 439.
2 Beer, 261.

The team approach to OR studies is almost universally accepted as one means of helping to reduce uncertainties in system problems. After they emphasized the team approach, George Creelman and Richard Wallen advocated the need for social scientists on mixed teams since:

> In addition to suggesting psychological variables, the psychologist will have ideas about measuring them....Social psychologists know something about overcoming irrational resistance to organizational change.[1]

The collection and analysis of the systems data

In sharp contrast with what can be and is done in many areas of science and mathematics, OR studies by necessity require the gathering of data before system solutions are attempted. While biochemists studying microchemical interactions or nuclear physicists studying subatomic particles are often forced to propound theoretical model constructs because of their relative inability to gather direct data, by contrast some mathematicians take special pride in the purity of their research, and purposely avoid any attempt to seek applied data or examples in their abstract studies.

---

1 George D. Creelman and Richard W. Wallen, "The Place of Psychology in Operations Research," Opns. Res., 6 (January-February, 1958), 119.

It is generally considered poor OR practice to attempt
a formulation of system patterns a priori. This is
due to the fact "... that the problems in the real
life environment are fraught with restrictions,
problems of data gathering, and, in particular,
require mixtures of techniques in their solution
that are seldom implied or indicated in OR literature."[1]

Once the system problem has been formulated, the
OR analyst must be concerned with gathering data, no
matter how crude, before proceeding to the modeling
stage. However,

> no pregnant problem should be left unattempted
> for lack of exact numerical data, for often
> it is found on doing the analysis that some
> significant conclusions recommending concrete
> action can be drawn even with very rough data.[2]

There is of course the opposite extreme viewpoint,
whereby the system problem is lost sight of through
an over zealous gathering of too much data.

> It is entirely possible to 'research hell' out
> of a problem, winding up with hundreds of charts,
> all prepared perfectly correctly and analyzed
> properly; but if the essential simplification
> which makes the problem understandable is missing,
> the work is relatively useless.[3]

1 R. P. Hypher, "Letter to the Editor," Opns. Res.,
11 (January-February, 1963), 154.
2 P. M. S. Blackett, "Operational Research," The
Advancement of Science, V, (April, 1948), 33.
3 Randels, 118.

Often the gathering of the proper data refocuses the entire OR study, as Arne Jensen has documented in the analysis of ship collisions at the only channel entrance to the Baltic Sea.[1] In 1940 the British Admiralty asked an OR team to design a gun that could be fired vertically because ship crews were unanimous in stating that enemy dive-bombers were attacking in a "vertical" direction.

> By placing an inconscpicuous grid on the wall of the interrogation room and asking the witness to point his hand in the direction of the aircraft, it was soon found that 'vertical' to a man being attacked was between 45° and 75°. This research saved us the task of overcoming very difficult design problems to produce a weapon which would have been of little value.[2]

OR analysts will often go to any extreme to gather data. During World War II, it was found that even slight surface irregularities reduced the effectiveness of artillery shells to only about twenty percent of their effective value on smooth terrain. An OR analyst

> ... found that if he used the poles that surveyors used he could stand on his head in the middle of an array of poles, read off the heights, and in that way measure the irregularities of the ground quantitatively.[3]

1 Arne Jensen, "Safety-at-Sea Problems," in the Proceedings of the Fourth International Conference on Operational Research, David B. Hertz and Jacques Melese, eds. (New York: Wiley-Interscience, 1966), 362-370.

2 Sir Charles Goodeve, "Operational Research," Nature, 161 (March 13, 1948), 380.

3 Omand Solandt, "Observation, Experiment, and Measurement in Operations Research," Opns. Res., 3 (February, 1955), 8.

The method turned out to be surprisingly effective but equally dangerous to the researcher who was jailed by London police after he was found "... standing on his head in the middle of Barnes Common and refused to say what he was doing except that it was highly secret."[1]

The question of secrecy and security is frequently encountered in military OR studies, and often in industrial and commercial OR studies as well. In the field of CJ, access to data as well as the OR study itself is sometimes a matter of secrecy and propriety for obvious reasons. "Problems of secrecy ... will nearly always obtrude in operations research in any field, and the worker must be prepared to cope with them intelligently and not emotionally."[2]

The search for appropriate model representations of the system

All the preceding steps are necessary preliminaries for the creation of an appropriate OR model representation of a system. The model is a "... fundamental conceptual device which enables one to regard the operation as a whole, ... [and] which attempts to establish a correspondence between the problem and rational thought..."[3] The language which the OR model

---

1 Solandt, 9.

2 Morse and Kimball, 7.

3 Saaty, 32.

uses

> ... is a metalanguage with respect to the
> network language of the practical situation
> [so that it is possible to]... discuss
> the situation which the model analogizes
> and ultimately maps, without being trapped
> into undecidable statements.[1]

The OR model ultimately assumes a mathematical
format since mathematics provides a logical, structured,
and rigorous language which tends to eliminate
uncertainties, and to effectively depict the problem
in unequivocal terminology readily suitable for
analysis and evaluation. However, it should not be
concluded that the use of mathematical modeling in
OR guarantees that the system study will be definitive, unequivocal, and without inadequacies.

Regardless of the mathematical complexity of
the analytical OR model, the underlying tenets are
usually of the following form.[2]

$$P = \oint_i f_i(x_j, y_k) \quad \text{subject to} \quad R_i .$$

Where:

P   is the total performance of the system under
study,

x_j are the variables of the system that can be
controlled and measured,

---

1   Beer, 208.

2   An expanded version of the presentation in,
Russell L. Ackoff and Maurice W. Sasieni, Fundamentals
of Operations Research, (New York: John Wiley & Sons,
Inc., 1968), 9.

y_k are the variables of the system that are
   not controllable and/or measurable, but do
   exert some effect on P,

f_i is the set of utility functions for each aspect
   of the problem, relating x_j, and hopefully y_k,
   to P,

$\cent_i$ is the combination of the separate functions f_i
   that must be considered to provide a valid
   representation of P,

R_i are the restrictions and constraints of the
   real system that must be considered in the
   formulations of the f_i functions.

Neither the symbolism nor the structure of the above
formulation should be interpreted to mean that a system
problem can be resolved if and only if it can be
represented in this form. In fact, this formulation
is actually a qualitative representation of OR modeling
methods despite its symbolic structure.

However , an over reliance on, or an unquestioned
use of mathematical modeling is to be avoided.
Otherwise, it would be too easy for the OR analyst
to construct purely theoretical model formulations,
and thereby to lose sight of the primary objective
of OR which is "... to try to substitute fact for
opinion in complex situations."[1]

---

1 Solandt, 6.

The construction of any OR model involves a highly delicate balance between the reality of the system being modeled and the artificiality of the model employed since, "... it may be difficult to create a model which is logically sound and which is also an empirically correct model of the desired content."[1] Nevertheless, M. L. Hurni contended that, "a crude but understandable model is preferable to a refined model that is not understood."[2] This apparent anomaly was probably best capsulated by R. P. Rich.

> When a complex situation is to be analyzed
> it is sometimes thought that the first step
> is the construction of a mathematical model.
> In practice, however, the construction of a
> mathematical model is far from the first step.
> By the time a really suitable model has been
> constructed in most cases, most of the hard
> work has already been done. Once the model
> has been constructed it can usually be analyzed
> and verified by standard techniques recorded in
> the literature and taught in recognized
> academic fields. The steps leading up to the
> model except for some concerned with the collec-
> tion of data, do not share these advantages.[3]

The use of an interdisciplinary team in the construction of an OR model is generally encouraged.

---

1 Stephen S. Willoughby, "Representations by Means of Formal Mathematical Structures," (Unpublished Ed.D. dissertation, Columbia University, 1961), 16.

2 M. L. Hurni, "Observations on Operations Research," Opns. Res., 2 (August, 1954), 242.

3 R. P. Rich, "Simulation as an Aid in Model Building," Opns. Res., 3 (February, 1955), 15.

> The principle of a mixed-team approach is
> simple and sound: by combining scientists
> from different disciplines on the same team,
> we increase the stimulation of new ideas and
> novel approaches and decrease the risk of
> neglecting important variables.[1]

However, the emphasis on the team of scientists, while

historically significant in OR's development during

World War II, is somewhat misplaced in most current

OR studies. The actual objective is not the team

itself, but the varied experiential backgrounds and

outlooks that each scientist brings to the OR study.

OR analysts have been known to leave no measure

untapped when seeking appropriate system models. Such

ingenuity is most apparent when the model tends to be

less symbolic and more physical in nature. J. G.

Crowther and R. Whiddington described a World War II

problem which required the determination of the optimum

wire diameter to be used to trip an alarm system when

Japanese troops crossed it. The trade-off involved

finding an appropriate wire diameter of high tensile

strength and low visibility, and then to determine the

proper height at which to string such a wire. The

British OR team solved the problem "... by stringing

wires across routes traversed by the large army of

women cleaners found in all Ministry of Supply establish-

ments either upright or on their knees with a scrubbing

---

1 Creelman and Wallen, 116.

brush."[1] The OR model so developed, correctly assumed
that the modes of observation and motion of the clean-
ing women would be typical of those of the Japanese
soldiers.

The manipulation of the model representations so as to obtain optimum system trade-offs

Once formulated, the model must demonstrate the
accuracy of its representation of the system. One way
of doing this is to manipulate the model in order to
determine how well it predicts optimum operating
levels of the system.

> It is this predictive capability which
> distinguishes the mathematical model, the
> theory, from a straightforward statistical
> analysis of observed data. The theory is an
> extrapolation; it has something more than
> past history: it has a hypothetical structure
> which can be checked by further experiment.[2]

Simply stated, the method of optimization involves
arriving at   controls, decisions, or solutions which
represent the most appropriate course of action to take
under certain specified or implied conditions and
constraints. Optimum results are functions of

1 J. G. Crowther and R. Whiddington, Science at War
(New York: Philosophical Library, 1948), 112.

2 Philip M. Morse, "Operational Research in the Public
Service," (paper presented at the Symposium on Opera-
tional Research, sponsored by the Organisation for
Economic Co-operation and Development, Dublin, Ireland,
September 29, 1965), 3.

circumstance, and as such must be constantly reevaluated. Frequently, optimization of a system or process only can be accomplished on its parts or subdivisions. Such a procedure is known as sub-optimization, and the results are not necessarily the total or global optimum for the system or process.

The search for optimum operation levels and solutions has led to the development of rather sophisticated OR methods such as linear programming, queueing theory, and simulation. These OR methodologies, and others, are used to obtain results which are designed to improve existing system operations and conditions in a perceptible, and demonstrable manner.

Nevertheless, "the OR man in real life ... finds that problems do not on the whole yield to these particular -- almost proprietary -- methods of solution."[1] Often it is inadvisable, impractical or impossible to obtain true optimum levels and solutions for complex system. "Frequently, because of lack of appropriate knowledge, excessive effort spent in producing an elaborate solution is not advisable."[2]

Hitch[3] has observed that OR analysts have been

---

1 Beer, 504.
2 Saaty, 28.
3 Charles Hitch, "Undertainties in Operations Research," 444.

overly obsessed with optimization both on the global
and the subsystem levels. The very nature of OR
modeling leads, in many cases, only to a close approximation of optimum levels and solutions of real
system problems.

> Operational research, with its inevitable
> compromises, is much more like an applied
> science, and may not suit those whose thoughts
> turn to purer paths. The actual work is
> largely a question of artifice and resource
> in the analysis and manipulation of the problems.[1]

The techniques of model manipulation used to find
optimum system solutions, vary from the analytical
method of evaluating a function's derivative at a
point, to the stochastic method of evaluating a
system's functioning through computer simulation.
Often, OR studies involve an artistic blend of
mathematical methods, mechanical models, and insight-
ful divinations in order to determine system optimums.

One such classical solution involved the analysis
of a special case of the traveling salesman problem
between forth-eight cities and Washington D. C. The
enumerative solution would have required checking
about 10^{61} possible routes which is far beyond present
computer capabilities. Yet, by clever simplifications,

---

1 Eric C. Williams, "Reflections on Operations Research,"
Opns. Res., 2 (November, 1954), 443.

imaginative intuition, and the use of pins and string,
an optimum solution was found by OR analysts.[1]

The examination of the accuracy, and the practicality
of the system optimums derived from the models

Since optimum system levels and solutions are
functions of circumstances such as inputs, outputs,
variables considered, reassignment of priority values,
model assumptions, and system limitations, results
obtained under one set of conditions are not necessarily valid at a later time even though the same set
of circumstances may appear to prevail. As illustrations of this, consider the outcomes of sporting
events between the same opponents on different
occasions, or the outbreak of crime waves in the
same city at different times.[2]

Consequently, it is necessary to monitor and
constantly check the results considered to be optimum
as obtained by OR model manipulations. Even systems
(such as a thermostatically controlled heating system),

1 Consult, G. Dantzig, D. R. Fulkerson, and S. M.
Johnson, "Solution of a Large-Scale Traveling-Salesman
Problem," Opns. Res., 2 (November-December, 1954), 393-
410.

2 Consult, Nelson B. Heller and Robert E. Markland,
"A Climatological Model for Forecasting the Demand
for Police Service " (paper presented at the 37th
national meeting of the Operations Research Society
of America, Washington D. C., April 20, 1970).

fitted with cybernetic feedback units (that is,
automatic error and adjustment controls, and
communications designed to reestablish system
equilibrium and normality after variations in
output optimality), must be reexamined because
the premises upon which the cybernetic feedback
was designed may no longer be valid.

Real life situations are often quite complicated, and as such, complete and exact descriptions
of their operations may defy even the best OR study.
All OR studies fall between a fairly thorough
description of a small part of a system's operations,
and an invariably imperfect description of its
entire operation. Because of such incompleteness,
all derived optimum system levels and solutions
must be reexamined before the implementation of an
OR study is undertaken.

There is of course, the tendency to accept a
first solution as the solution. OR analysts must
guard against the temptation that

> sooner or later, the model and all its
> trappings, so essential to actual progress,
> may begin to dominate truth. ... Progress in
> science might well be defined as the overthrow
> of a model, and its appurtenances, that [have]
> exhausted [their] usefulness.[1]

As an illustration of the importance of checking

---

1 Beer, 122.

"solutions," consider the following problem that
occurred during World War II. The problem involved
the optimum location and amount of armour plate to
be placed on allied bombers so as to reduce plane
loss from ground gun flak. The trade-off was fairly
obvious since a completely armoured plane increased
fuel consumption while decreasing bomb load capacity,
whereas an unarmoured plane was totally susceptible
to flak attack but had a high bomb load capacity.

It was decided to model the solution based on
an analysis of the flak holes of seventy of one
hundred bombers that had returned from a bombing
mission. The analysis was begun, and its recommendations undoubtedly would have been implemented had not
Morse questioned the model hypothesis. Morse observed
that it would probably be optimal to place the armour
around the flak holes of the planes that had not
returned![1] It was only after the war that captured
German documents revealed an appropriate means of
resolving the problem for future aircraft design.[2]

1 Crowther and Whiddington, 108.

2 Consult, Theodore Benecke, "Methods of Air Defence
Over Germany in World War II," in Operational Research
in Practice, ed. by Max Davies and Michel Verhulst
(London: Pergamon Press, 1958), 72-85. This study
also dispels the widely held belief that there was no
OR type activity in the German military during
World War II.

The communication and implementation of the
model optimums into the system

Once OR methods have determined optimum levels
and solutions, there still remains a need to communicate these results to the system personnel, and
implement the recommended changes into system
operations. However, there seems to be no universally
accepted standard of how to proceed since "... the
references that are made to the practical usage of
the model and solution are very vague and general,
and imply that implementation follows in the normal
course of the operations to which the study has been
applied."[1] This rarely occurs because "proper
implementation of a solution to a problem is perhaps
still more an art than a science."[2]

Nevertheless, some OR analysts minimize the
importance of the implementation phase as a necessary
and integral part of an OR study. Their position is
based on the belief that an OR analyst must maintain
an impartiality, and an independence from the system
under study so as not to jeopardize his personal
integrity and objectivity. Thus, from this viewpoint,
an OR study is viewed as "... a recommendation for

---

1 Paul Stillson, "Implementation of Problems in O.R.,"
Opns. Res., 11 (January-February, 1963), 140.
2 Russel L. Ackoff, "The Development of Operations
Research as a Science," Opns. Res., 4 (June, 1956), 287.

action and is not in itself, a plan of action.
In fact, ... operations research must not accept
any direct authority or responsibility for action..."[1]

The difficulties surrounding proper implementation of OR studies stem from a variety of sources.
One of the most prominent, as pointed out by Russell
L. Ackoff,[2] is that OR solutions are usually implemented by system managers whose mathematical sophisti-
cation leaves much to be desired. Whenever such
circumstances prevail, it is fairly safe to assume
that the acceptance of OR studies by executives
must depend principally upon successful demonstra-
tions of performance more than a clear understanding
of the techniques employed. Ackoff also observed
that this often forces the OR team to "... either
translate elegant solutions into approximations
that are easy to use, or sidestep the elegance and
move directly to a quick-and-dirty decision-rule."[3]

There also must be a cooperative and trusted

1 Ellis A. Johnson, "The Executive, the Organization,
and Operations Research," in Operations Research for
Management, Vol. I, J. F. McCloskey and F. N. Trefethen,
eds. (Baltimore: The Johns Hopkins Press, 1966), xxiii.

2 Ackoff, "The Development of Operations Research
as a Science," 287.

3 Ibid.

alliance between the OR team and the system
managers in order to execute proper implementation
of an OR study. In the various compromises that
must be made, one of the responsibilities of the
OR team is to see to it that as little loss of
solution effectiveness as possible, is incurred
during the implementation and communication phase
of the OR study. In bridging this gap between OR
theory and managerial policy the OR analyst "... must
be careful, on the one hand, not to qualify his
study out of existence or, on the other hand, to
assume the prerogatives of the executive and decide
what is best."[1]

Consider the following example as an illustration
of just how difficult proper implementation can be even
when the solution is quite clearly defined.

> ... I noticed a home just down the street from
> mine burning up one night and called the fire
> department which said, 'Yes, we know.' Still it
> was at least twenty minutes before a truck
> arrived although the station was certainly less
> than ten minutes away. The house was completely
> destroyed. It turned out later that many other
> neighbors had called -- several well before I had.
> We finally decided the fire truck could not get
> away because the phone kept ringing.[2]

John W. Abrams[3] has reported that unimplemented
OR studies were found to emphasize physical variables

---

1 Ware, 8.

2 Alex M. Mood, "Diversification of Operations Research,"
Opns. Res., 13 (March-April, 1965), 176-177.

3 John W. Abrams, "Implementation of Operational Research:
A Problem in Sociology," The Journal of the Canadian
Operational Research Society, 3 (November, 1965), 152-160.

more frequently, and tended to avoid those
variables that related human reactions to environmental and social change.

The reevaluation and adjustment of the implemented optimums
through regular system monitoring and feedback analysis

The need to reevaluate and adjust implemented
optimals through regular system monitoring is not at
all discussed in the current OR literature. Yet when
dealing with dynamic and complex systems such as the
CJ system, such a requirement is mandatory. Just as
no OR model solution is permanently optimum, so it
is that no implemented solution can remain optimum
over a given time period.

This requirement for reevaluation and adjustment
of implemented optimums can be accomplished in some
instances through

> ... error-regularing negative feedbacks that
> directly reduce the powers allowed to a
> wandering variable, and indirectly force
> it back to its acknowledged best level.
> But it has also been shown that feedback
> must operate on the entire structure of
> whatever proliferates variety, on its organi-
> zation, [and] on the built-in sub-systems that
> produce aberrant behavior.[1]

At present it seems most practical for most system
managers to commission periodic OR studies rather than
to insist on regular reevaluations of previous OR
studies. To this end, many companies do have regular
OR divisions; and New York City for example,has a
Criminal Justice Coordinating Council as well as an OR
study unit.

1 Beer, 301.

CHAPTER IV

POTENTIAL PITFALLS IN OPERATIONS RESEARCH STUDIES

Just as in any other discipline, OR has its fair
share of pitfalls which often arise from a misappli-
cation of its basic methodology and philosophy. The
following presentation represents a cross section of
some actual and potential pitfalls in the application of OR. They are discussed here in the hope that
CJ professionals will, for the most part, profit by
the mistakes of their predecessors in OR.

One of the first OR pitfalls to be identified
was based on a case described by Morse and Kimball.
During World War II "an operations research worker
during his first day of assignment to a new field
command noticed that there was considerable delay
caused by the soldiers having to wait in line to wash
and rinse their mess kits after eating."[1] Of the
four tubs, two were used for washing and two for
rinsing. The OR analyst observed that the average
soldier took three times longer washing his mess kit

---

1 Philip M. Morse and George E. Kimball, Methods of
Operations Research (1st ed. rev.; Cambridge, Mass.:
The M.I.T. Press, 1970), 3.

than rinsing it. In traditional OR style, the
analyst accepted the limiting constraint of four
tubs (that is, he assumed he could not obtain
additional tubs), and suggested that three should
be used for washing and only one for rinsing.
"This change was made, and the line of waiting
soldiers did not merely diminish in size; on most
days no waiting line ever formed."[1] Morse and
Kimball conceded that this illustration of an OR
study was trivial, that the solution once seen was
absurdly simple, and that it seemed amazing that
a trained scientist was needed to point out a
solution.

When Alex Mood reviewed the Morse and Kimball
text, however, he quoted the following "verbatim
account" from the mess sergeant about the OR
analyst's worth.

> Yeah, I remember that guy. He had some
> screwball idea that the mission of the Army
> was to eliminate waiting lines. Actually I
> had it all figured out that two was the right
> number of rinse tubs. With everyone rinsing
> in one tub the bacteria count would get way
> past the critical level. But we switched to
> one rinse tub while he was around because the
> old man says he's an important scientist or
> something and we got to humor him. Had damn
> near a third of the outfit out with the belly-
> ache before we got the character off the
> reservation. Then we quick switched to three
> rinse tubs and really made a nice line.

---

1 Morse and Kimball, 3.

> 'Nothing like a good line to get the men's
> legs in condition,' the old man says. He
> was right too. Six months later during
> Patton's dash across France we got stuck
> with a 30-mile cross-country hike to cut
> off a highway. The boys were in top shape
> and went the whole way in high gear.[1]

Even though this mess sergeant's account is completely fabricated, as Mood stated: "I regret (?) to report that the verbatim account of the mess sergeant was pure invention. I must have been in a mischievous mood when I wrote that review."[2] Nevertheless, it still illustrated several potential pitfalls and fallacies that OR studies must guard against. No aspect of a problem is too trivial and no solution is so obvious that the OR analyst can choose to ignore:

1. gathering all the reasons for a current practice or procedure,

2. seeking the advice of the personnel most directly involved with implementing the current practice,

3. consulting the personnel who will be affected by a change in procedure, and

1 Alex M. Mood, review of Methods of Operations Research, by Philip M. Morse and George E. Kimball, in Opns. Res., 1 (November, 1953), 307.

2 Letter from Alex M. Mood, Ph.D., Director of the Public Policy Research Organization, University of California at Irvine, dated Irvine, Calif., April 1, 1971.

4. considering the consequences of a feasible solu-
    tion before attempting its implementation.

The lesson in this pitfall might well be applied
to District Attorneys and Judges, who, when faced
with large case backlogs, overloaded court calendars,
and crowded prisons, select the expediencies of
reducing the charges against accused criminals, grant-
ing lighter sentences to convicted criminals, forcing
through quick verdicts, short-circuiting legal
guarantees, or failing to apply judicial safeguards.
The delays may thus be reduced, but does this trade-off
in justice versus time protect the rights of society
or provide equal treatment for those brought to trial?

Another pitfall was reported by Omond Solandt
whose World War II OR section was asked by the
British artillery command to examine gun drills and
suggest means of improvement. The OR study was able
to demonstrate that only three men rather than six
were required to effectively operate an antitank gun.
Unfortunately, the study had not considered the
gunners' needs. When the final report was passed on
to the gunners their response was direct.

> We never use more than three men in action,
> but we have been working for twenty years
> with the War Establishment Committee to get
> enough men in the organization to do the cook-
> ing, to bring up the ammunication, and to go
> scrounging around for supplies for the officers

> mess etc., and here you are showing us
> how we can get rid of these men. Burn
> the report![1]

Solandt's group did just that.

The lesson of this pitfall might very well be applied, for example, to those CJ studies which seek to cut costs by reducing the number of correctional personnel through an increase in the number of convicts held under maximum security conditions, or improve police patrol by using one policeman in a patrol car rather than two. The cost cuts might be accomplished, but at what price to the rehabilitation of the convicts, and their readjustment to society upon release? Similarly, there may be more areas patrolled but at what personal risk to the patrolmen involved, and with what measurable increase in effectiveness?

Even a thorough gathering of expert opinion from the users of a system does not eliminate one potential pitfall, namely, that the practitioners themselves may not fully understand the system, or that they are not objective enough to evaluate it. An illustration of this type of pitfall occurred early in World War II when British tanks, which had previously been knocking out German tanks at quite long range in Libya, were

---

1 Omand Solant, "Observation, Experiment, and Measurement in Operations Research," Opns. Res., 3 (February, 1955), 3.

suddenly and inexplicably being knocked out themselves.
It was· thought that "... the Germans had introduced
into service a new tank gunsight of colossal dimen-
sions."[1] The British gunners decided that this was the
cause of their defeats, and that·their gunsights should
be improved.

The OR study showed that, in fact, the British
were still hitting the tanks, but due to the facts
that their ammunition was not equipped with penetrat-
ing caps, and that the Germans were using harder
armour, the shells were bouncing off the German tanks
unnoticed by the British gunners. Thus, "the
complaint of the users bore no relationship to the
cause of the trouble and at the time no one understood
the tank gun weapons system well enough to say
immediately that their complaint was obviously
misstated."[2] It was not until all aspects of the tank
gun weapon system, including those of gunner control
and behavior were carefully studied, that the OR
analysts were able to resolve the problem.

The implications in this pitfall seem readily
applicable to those police chiefs and politicians who

---

1 Solandt, 12.
2 Ibid.

assume that an increase in police manpower or
equipment alone will serve to reduce crime rates.
The trade-offs required for the balancing of costs
against results does not merely revolve around one
agency within the CJ system, but, in fact, must
encompass all agencies of the CJ system in order
to be fully effective.

In the calculation of expected values or
utilities used to develop measure matrices, it is
often necessary to assume the independence of certain
probabilities, and to assume that strategies are to
be selected against neutral states of nature. To
illustrate the potential fallacies in such assumptions, Hitch reported a letter from a Barbados bricklayer requesting sick leave from his employer.

> RESPECTED SIR, when I got to the building,
> I found that the hurricane had knocked some
> bricks off the top. So I rigged up a beam
> with a pulley at the top of the building and
> hoisted up a couple of barrels full of bricks.
> When I had fixed the building, there was a lot
> of bricks left over.
>
> I hoisted the barrel back up again and secured
> the line at the bottom, and then went up and
> filled the barrel with extra bricks. Then I
> went to the bottom and cast off the line.
>
> Unfortunately, the barrel of bricks was heavier
> than I was and before I knew what was happening
> the barrel started down, jerking me off the
> ground. I decided to hang on and halfway up
> I met the barrel coming down and received a
> severe blow on the shoulder.

I then continued to the top, banging my head
against the beam and getting my finger jammed
in the pulley. When the barrel hit the ground
it bursted its bottom, allowing all the bricks
to spill out.

I was heavier than the barrel and so started
down again at high speed. Halfway down, I
met the barrel coming up and received severe
injuries to my shins. When I hit the ground
I landed on the bricks, getting several painful
cuts from the sharp edges.

At this point I must have lost my presence of
mind, because I let go to the line. The barrel
then came down giving me another heavy blow on
the head and putting me in the hospital.[1]

Considering every action and decision described
by the bricklayer as an event with binary outcomes
(for example, he either hangs on to the rope or lets
it go, and he receives an injury or he does not), it
is possible to obtain a crude estimate of the theoretical probability for such a sequence of contingent
events to have occurred. There are, by count, at least
twenty binary actions and decisions described in the
letter. Thus, the probability for such a set of
tandem outcomes is:

$$P \leq \frac{1}{2^{20}} = \frac{1}{1,048,576}$$

That is, there is less than one chance in a million
of such an occurrence when each outcome is considered

1 Charles Hitch, "Uncertainties in Operations
Research," Opns. Res., 8 (July-August, 1960), 440-441.

independent of the preceding ones. However, because of the interdependence of events (which are not always so obvious as they are in this case), theoretical probability values can be misleading, if not outright inaccurate even when conditional probabilities are taken into account.

The import of this last pitfall can be vital to the documentation of trial evidence by the forensic scientist. The string of clues linking a suspect to a crime must be unbroken, as well as the investigative chain that handled the evidence. The probability for doubting a positive identification of the suspect must be negligible or essentially zero if a convication is to be obtained. Inevitably, there is always the delicate balance between the admissibility of evidence, the adequacy of the evidential findings, the interdependence of the clues, and the subjective treatment of the documentation by the jurors, which must be considered by the forensic scientist if he is to avoid the pitfall described above.[1]

A rather subtle pitfall may arise when OR studies are taken too seriously, and they are assumed to provide ultimate solutions under all conditions, rather than

---

1 Consult, Charles R. Kingston, "Probability and Legal Proceedings," The Journal of Criminal Law, Criminology and Police Science, 57 (March, 1966), 93-98.

optimum solutions under specified constraints,
which should be subjected to periodic reevaluations.
Some classical OR models, such as those in queueing
theory are designed primarily to analyze and to
characterize the nature of the problem, and rarely
therefore, provide direct optimum solutions by
themselves.

With these statements in mind, it should be easier
to appreciate H. F. Ellis' sarcastic barbs of humor
directed at the British Operational Research Society's
investigation of bus delays using OR queueing theory.

> It is a great comfort, waiting here for a No. 11,
> to know that the matter is in hand. [They are
> using]... 'methods which were used in the war to
> improve antisubmarine and antiaircraft defenses,'
> ... [to study] the problem of why buses on certain
> routes in London are unable to force a way
> through to their successive objectives except
> in concentrations of a dozen or more.[1]

> The fault from which the No. 11 route suffers,
> it has been discovered, is 'dynamic instability'
> [the major cause of which is due to time lost
> in traffic jams]... Spectacular proof of the
> correctness of this theory has been afforded
> by the recent acute petrol shortage, when it
> was shown that, with less traffic on the streets,
> buses ran more regularly.[2]

1 H. F. Ellis, "Written in a Queue," Opns. Res., 6
(January-February, 1958), 125.

2 Ibid., 126.

The implications of this pitfall permeate almost all OR studies of the CJ system. Because of the dynamic nature of the CJ system, and the fact that the CJ system is only partially understood, most OR studies on the CJ system or any of its components amount to the analyses of data, the organization of information, the tracing of system flows, or the procedural identifications which tend, at best, to pinpoint potential bottlenecks and identify aspects to which resources should be directed, without actually being able to offer solutions. An excellent example of a thorough study of police apprehension practices that was of necessity unable to offer suggested improvements capable of immediate implementation was illustrated in a recent RAND Institute study.[1]

A potential source of pitfalls that must be contended with in OR studies arises from the very nature of the problems undertaken. Unlike pure mathematical or scientific studies which can often isolate a small, specific, and independent part of a problem for investigation, OR studies, no matter how narrowly defined, must consider all aspects of

---

1 Consult, Peter W. Greenwood, An Analysis of the Apprehension Activities of the New York City Police Department, RAND Corp. Report R-529-NYC (New York: The New York City RAND Institute, September, 1970).

the problem or risk a superficial analysis of it. It is this characteristic that Hitch claimed, with some degree of apology, that distinguishes OR from the other sciences.[1]

Almost paradoxically however, because the realities of most systems are so complex, OR studies must be geared to a manageable portion of the entire system in a manner that somehow still considers its totality without complicating the analysis of the subsystem under study. Such a trade-off between reality and manageability in the OR study of systems is accomplished by means of suboptimization.

Hitch was the first to suggest that the analysis of complex systems must be accomplished through the process of suboptimization. "Sub-optimization is this process of choosing among a relatively small number of alternatives by an administrative level other than the highest."[2] To be successful the OR study must be cut down to workable size at the lower level. However, the OR analyst can only "... reach valid and useful conclusions by choosing with care criteria that are consistent with objectives at higher levels."[3]

---

1 Charles Hitch, "Comments," Opns. Res., 4 (August, 1956), 426.

2 Charles Hitch, and Roland McKean, "Suboptimization in Operations Research," in Operations Research for Management, Vol. I, J. F. McCloskey and F. N. Trefethen, eds. (Baltimore: The Johns Hopkins Press, 1966), 172.

3 Hitch, "Comments," 430.

The fallacy lies in the fact that the task of
suboptimization must unavoidably be applied in OR
studies, but such a procedure "... will not automatically reveal optimal choices [and in fact,]...
may give worse results than the flipping of coin."[1]
This fallacy essentially amounts to the traditional
admonition against extrapolating results beyond the
range of limited data, yet paradoxically most OR
studies require such extrapolations as the only
feasible course of action.

That suboptimization is a necessary procedure
in the OR analysis of complex problems is undisputed.
However, its improper application leads to a common
dilemma. Simply stated, it amounts to the fact that
the global or overall optimal for a system does not
necessarily result from a combination of all the
suboptimal values. "The usual procedure for handling
combined processes consists of 'solving' them in
sequence. Even with successive cyclic adjustments
we know that in many cases we fail to get a true
optimum."[2] What makes matters even worse is that as
more of a system's components are incorporated in

---

1 Hitch and McKean, 172.

2 Russell L. Ackoff, "The Development of Operations
Research as a Science," Opns. Res., 4 (June, 1956),
285.

the search for a global optimal, the order of
difficulty in obtaining it increases rapidly, with a
simultaneous rapid decrease in the competence of OR
methods available to handle the search. However, the
OR analyst "... need not solve global problems in all
their complexity in order to recognize their features,
a happy circumstance which makes useful OR possible."[1]

Another potential pitfall arises when the OR
analyst assumes that his work is concluded once the
model has been formulated so that an appropriate set
of decisions can be selected from it. Due to the
nature of most OR problems and their solutions, a
constant monitoring and up dating of model-derived
solutions is necessary. In fact, optimization is by
its nature a function of circumstance, and therefore
does not necessarily bear any finality or appropriateness beyond the time-data construct in which it was
first formulated. The pitfall of assuming a lack of
continuity in time, which can be as fallacious as the
disregard for the spatial relationships between the
parts of a system when suboptimizing, fails to consider
that future decisions are dependent on present actions
and decisions.

---

1 Hitch, "Comments," 430.

Of course, there are mathematical pitfalls and
fallacies which are particularly inherent to OR studies
that are just as dangerous as those pitfalls based
on methodological and philosophical considerations.
Mathematical pitfalls often tend to be more difficult
to discover, and to correct, due to the mistaken
belief that once a problem is placed into a symbolic
model or quantified format its solution is immune from
errors. Although such immunity is usually valid for
the standard OR model itself, it is far from valid
for the underlying assumptions and conditions upon
which the OR model itself is structured, and ultimately
from which the solution is derived. In OR studies,
if the underlying assumptions and restrictions are
ignored or treated lightly, then the derived model
may have been designed to solve the wrong problem.

B. O. Koopman warned against four common mathematical pitfalls and fallacies in OR modeling, which
he defined as follows.

>Linearitis is the assumption that every
>function is linear, and that simple propor-
>tion is the measure of all things.
>
>Maximitis is the mental condition leading to
>the assumption that the most probable thing
>will happen; and, since the average is often
>the most probable value, the belief in its
>virtual certainty.
>
>Mechanitis is the occupational disease of one
>who is so impressed with modern computing
>machinery that he believes that a mathematical
>problem, which he can neither solve nor even
>formulate, can readily be answered, once he

has access to a sufficiently expensive
machine.

Authorititis is that regression to logical
infantilism which believes that the missing
links in one's solution of a problem, as well
as the missing common sense required for
relating it to reality, can be readily
supplied by the uniformed officer or the
company executive who must eventually use
the result.[1]

In addition, there are those fallacies that
afflict the analysis of problems by OR methods due to
an overreliance on mathematics. Such potential fallacies arise because as a supplement to the necessary
mathematical and experimental science input that must
go into OR modeling, there is a need for that all
important "... working version of the concept of value,
with all its human and practical overtones."[2] It is
a firm understanding of the concept of value that
forms the basis for establishing criteria for judging
model appropriateness, for assigning priorities to
the variables of a model, for providing the measure
matrices of a model, and for measuring model effectiveness. Attempts at deriving such subtle model
considerations as value from

... the methods of the classical (indirect)
school of the calculus of variations, [and
similar]... formalisms are deceptive. The

---

1 B. O. Koopman, "Fallacies in Operations Research,
Opns. Res., 4 (August, 1956), 424.

2 Ibid., 423.

real OR problem, which commences with
dealing with the client and shaping up
the problem, is of course, omitted [from
such analyses]. Presumably this is attributable to mathematical license.[1]

It should be obvious that not all of potential
pitfalls inherent to OR studies have been discussed
here. Though not discussed here, those more standard
pitfalls and fallacies which tend to be common to all
scientific disciplines, must be carefully safeguarded
against by the OR and CJ analyst alike.[2] Typical of
this latter group would be the potential pitfalls
arising from:

1. a lack of accuracy in measuring input and
   output data,

2. a lack of precision in dealing with data,

3. a lack of dimensional analysis within
   the model, and

4. a lack of proper restraint in drawing
   conclusions from limited models, data
   and analyses.

---

1 A. Charnes and W. W. Cooper, "Such Solutions are Very
Little Solved," Opns. Res., 3 (August, 1955), 345.

2 Consult, Darrell Huff, How to Lie with Statistics,
(New York: W. W. Norton & Co., Inc., 1954).

PART II

THE MATHEMATICAL MODELS OF

OPERATIONS RESEARCH

CHAPTER V

THE CONCEPT OF MODELING

Models are ubiquitous. Almost all aspects of
human endeavor involve modeling of some sort. As far
back as the civilizations of ancient Babylonia and
China, astronomers sought to model the solar system
in order to describe and predict the complexities of
the heavens. The concept of modeling is crucial to
most scientific pursuits, and is particularly central
to the study of the CJ system through OR methods.

Simply stated, a model is a representation
designed to describe, to explain and to predict, as
realistically as possible, the essential aspects of
a concept, device, process, or system. The model is
structured around certain assumptions from which, by
specified rules of inference, it depicts an idealiza-
tion intended to approximate the complex reality
accurately, yet, is much easier to understand and
utilize.

A model is especially necessary when the system
it seeks to represent is too complex to be dealt with
in its entirety, and/or when the system is only

partially understood. A model is rarely needed to
appreciate the complexity of a system, but it
certainly is needed to represent its functioning,
and to attempt controls or improvements in its operations. In more pragmatic terms, the overwhelming
complexity of the study of systems is only made
reasonable through the development of appropriate
representations based on simplifying models. The
entire scientific method can be viewed as a pursuit
for optimality through the creation, modification,
correction, and improvement of feasible model
solutions.

The early view of modeling was based almost
exclusively on Sir Isaac Newton's "Law of Similarity."
That is, the model had to maintain the geometric
and dynamic equivalencies of the reality being modeled.
Such essentially "scale-model" approaches to dealing
with reality showed their limitations most graphically
when physicists began to probe into the nature of
subatomic particles. The rejection of modeling under
such exclusively restrictive fetters was an essential
step in bringing new modeling forms to bear on problems
in economics, social processes, system interactions,
and complex physical phenomena, that previously had
been superficially studied due to the lack of
appropriate modeling methods.

It should be noted that all models must be
expressed in some language, as a representation of
the thoughts of the model formulator. Due to the
many ambiguities of the written language, and the
restrictions of the concrete scale-model, it is easy
to appreciate the relatively recent and rapid rise
of symbolic and mathematical modeling as evidenced
by the developments in mathematical physics, biology,
economics, and the social sciences. However, the true
system reality may still lie outside the language of
the model, no matter how mathematically abstract the
theoretic construct.[1] Thus, the most refined model
is more than likely just an imperfect reflection of
the complex reality it is designed to represent.

The **cla**ssification of models can be as varied
as the uses to which they are put. They may vary
from the qualitative or descriptive models, to the
quantitative or normative models. The ultimate
objective of any system model is to have its design
as quantitatively close as possible to reality so that
it will not only describe the reality, but also will
provide measurable evidence of its precision, and

---

1 Consult, Kurt Gödel, On Undecidable Propositions of
Formal Mathematical Systems (Princeton: Princeton
University Press, 1934).

predictive values. Indeed, a common measure of how
"advanced" a scientific discipline is often lies in
the status of its quantifiable models.[1]

Almost anything can, and almost everything has
been modeled in one form or another. However, the
process of modeling is not an end in itself. Once
established, the model is manipulated so that it can
be determined how the reality it is designed to
represent will respond to various and changing conditions. The ability to manipulate a model rather than
to have to deal with the total reality results in an
obvious saving of time, effort, money, and resources.

The model must respond to its input patterns in
a manner sufficiently close to the system reality it
is designed to represent. Essentially, the precision
of its imitation defines a model's accuracy, appropriateness, and predictive value. Observed discrepancies
between the model and the system reality are used as
a basis to modify the model. Eventually, the model
may even have to be discarded if the sufficient and
necessary adjustments needed to restore its realism
become unmanageable so that the model becomes useless.

1 Consult, Olaf Helmar and Nicholas Rescher, "On the
Epistemology of the Inexact Sciences," Management
Science, 6 (October, 1959), 25-52.

Formula Models

Formulas relating a dependent variable explicitly
to one or more independent variables are rare in OR
modeling of the CJ system. In fact, if such formulas
do exist for the modeling of certain aspects of a
system, then it is unlikely that the methods of OR
would be required in the analysis. However, a few
formulas that might be of some value to CJ professionals
are presented here for illustrative purposes.

Conrad Rizer[1] developed an explicit formula useful
in forensic science to determine the length of time (t)
in hours, that a corpse has been dead. A modification
of that formula follows.

$$t = (t_2-t_1) \frac{\log (T_B-T_0) - \log (T_1-T_0)}{\log (T_1-T_0) - \log (T_2-T_0)}$$

Where:

T_B equals normal rectal body temperature,

T_0 equals the temperature of the surroundings,

T_1 equals the first rectal temperature taken on
the corpse,

T_2 equals the second rectal temperature taken
on the corpse,

1 Conrad Rizer, "Police Mathematics," (unpublished
Ed.D. dissertation, New York University, 1950),
108-112.

t_1 equals the time of the first rectal temperature reading, and

t_2 equals the time of the second rectal temperature reading.

Nelson A. Watson[1] developed an elaborate formula for measuring crime (C), as a function of its amount (a), its type (t), and its severity (s), over a large number of independent variables. Unfortunately, no attempt was made to describe how to measure most of the variables presented, nor was there any indication of the weights assigned to each of the variables. As an explicit formula it is worthless, but as an aid in viewing law enforcement as a system, and as an aid in relating the relative effects of a large number of CJ variables in a qualitative manner it is excellent. The formula follows as presented, without the detailed explanations that accompanied each variable.

$$C_{a,t,s} = \frac{(L)(O)(I+D+N)(A)(R)}{PA_c + (SC + P_uO_p + P_uC_n) + (S_pT + EC_r) - (P_1P_r + PC_p) - ip + Oj}$$

Where:

L   represents legislation,

O   represents opportunity,

I   represents intent,

D   represents desire,

1 Nelson A. Watson, "Police Philosophy: A Formula for Crime," <u>The Police Chief</u>, XXXIV (September, 1967), 10-11,14,16.

N   represents negligence,

A   represents the act,

R   represents responsibility,

PA_c represents police activity,

SC   represents self control,

P_uO_p represents public opinion,

P_uC_n represents public cooperation,

S_pT represents a speedy trial,

EC_r represents effective correction,

P_lP_r represents political protection,

PC_p represents police corruption,

ip   represents interaction potential, and

Oj   represents good (social) order with justice.

It is a fairly well accepted principle among
sociologists, that as the number of people increases
in a given community, with other factors remaining
constant, the likelihood for human interaction
potential[1] and therefore, criminal activity, increases.
By means of elementary combinatorial mathematics, it
is evident that for n people the number of interactions
between pairs of people is given by $_nC_2$, which equals
$\frac{n(n-1)}{2}$. The number of interactions, along with the
corresponding potential for crime increases quadrati-
cally with n as the following table indicates.

---

1 Watson, 14,16.

Number of People·	n	2	3	4	5	...	10	...	100	...	n
Number of People-Pair Interactions	$_nC_2$	1	3	6	10	...	45	...	4950	...	$\frac{n^2-n}{2}$

Such people-pair interactions are referred to
frequently in the literature. An aspect of human
interaction that has been overlooked however, is the
sum total potential of   people-n-tuple interactions
that are possible among n people. That is, given n
people, in how many ways can they combine to commit
crimes against their neighbors. For example, given
three people A, B, and C, the following table summarizes the twelve total number of possible criminal
coalitions among the three people.

Criminal Perpetrator(s)	A	A	A	B	B	B	C	C	C	AB	AC	BC
Criminal Victim(s)	B	C	B,C	A	C	A,C	A	B	A,B	C	B	A

The following formula will provide the total
number of potential crime interactions (T) for n
people combining in i coalitions from i = 1 to i=n-1.

$$T = \sum_{i=1}^{n-1} {}_nC_i (2^{n-i} - 1)$$

For n = 4, the formula yields fifty potential crime
interaction combinations, as follows:

$$T = \sum_{i=1}^{4-1} {}_4C_i \ (2^{4-i} - 1)$$

$$= {}_4C_1 \ (2^3 - 1) + {}_4C_2 \ (2^2 - 1) + {}_4C_3 \ (2^1 - 1)$$

$$= (4)(7) + (6)(3) + (4)(1)$$

$$= 28 + 18 + 4$$

$$= 50 \ .$$

The following table indicates how much more rapidly the exponential nature of T increases with n as compared to the quadratic nature of ${}_nC_2$. The implications for CJ administrators, and the potential effect on the operations of law enforcement agencies, particularly in large cities, should be obvious.

Number of People	(n)	2	3	4	5	...	10	...	n
Total Number of Crime Potential Interaction Coalitions	(T)	2	12	50	180	...	57,002	...	$\sum_{i=1}^{n-1} {}_nC_i (2^{n-i}-1)$

Black Box Models

All modeling is ultimately a form of black box modeling. This is due to the fact that all systems to be modeled have certain unknown, uncertain, unmeasurable, or unfathomable aspects inherently associated with them. The process of modeling involves developing as precise a description of a system's characteristics

and operations as the observations, data, and knowledge
of the system will permit. As used here, the black
box model will be limited to a qualitative model format,
consisting of the objectives of the model, the inputs,
the outputs, and the feedback loops.

The term black box was coined early this century
by electrical engineers who found it convenient to set
up laboratory test experiments of the following nature.
Assume that there is a black box that contains an
unknown electrical circuit. The only access to the
black box is through a set of input and output terminals.
The problem is to determine the "nature" of the circuit
strictly by the application of known electrical
impulses at the input stage, and then to make measurements based on these inputs at the output terminals.
The resulting data must of course, be compared with
the behavior of known circuit components and their
various combinations. The objective of the test is
to determine the operational nature of the circuit
only, rather than its exact electrical composition,
since different circuits can produce the same measurable
electrical changes. For example, the voltage drop
across a direct current circuit of 40 ohms would
measure the same as the voltage drop across either a
series circuit of 30 ohms and 10 ohms, or a parallel
circuit of two 80 ohm resistors.

The black box modeling process is more practical than it might appear to be however, and in some instances no other modeling method is practical or possible. Consider the black box model in Figure 1 which is typical of most classroom educational procedures.

THE BLACK BOX

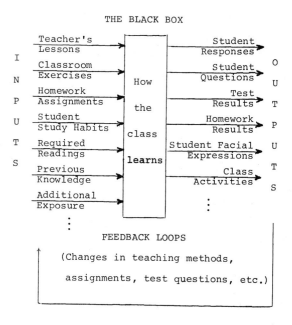

Fig. 1 -- A black box model of "how a class learns."

No teacher actually knows how all the students in the class learn, what their thoughts are, or why certain patterns of behavior and reaction are produced, when a lesson is presented. Certain inputs are supplied to the class, and because the teacher cannot enter the brain of any of the students, the teacher must depend upon a set of outputs to gauge the success of the instruction. The outputs are in turn used by the teacher to modify or adjust the inputs so as to improve the measured outputs according to some established criteria of merit that the teacher and students have set. This feedback process can take the form of rephrasing questions, changing homework assignments, providing additional readings, or adjusting the lecture-Socratic-discovery blend of the lesson. The set of input and output terminals are equivalent for the teacher and students alike -- the five senses. Unfortunately, most education in the typical school setting involves only two of these senses -- sight and hearing.

The four necessary parts of the black box model can now be outlined as follows, and are illustrated in Figure 2:

1. inputs -- those items that most immediately are essential to the activation and/or functioning of the black box,

2. outputs -- those items that are most immediately
attributable to the black box and its characterizations,

3. feedback loops -- a means of adjusting, modifying,
controlling, or monitoring the system in order to
change the inputs so as to provide operating levels
consistent with the desired outputs,

4. black box -- the unknown or unexplainable reality
which is to be described or classified principally
by the study of the system's input-output-feedback
relationships.

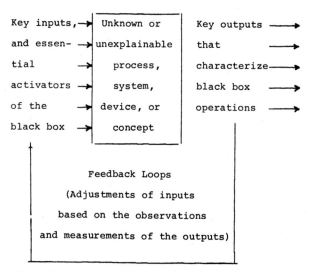

Fig. 2 -- A generalized black box model

It is common to treat most machines as black
box models when describing their operations. The
operations of a typewriter, an automobile, a
computer, a duplicating unit, or a gas chromato-
graph, are generally treated as black box phenomena.
Specified inputs are supplied in order to obtain the
desired outputs. If the outputs are unsatisfactory,
such as a misspelled word, an excessive speed, an
incomplete printout, a fuzzy copy, or an undistinguish-
able reading, the feedback loop principle is applied
in an attempt to adjust or to correct the inputs, so
as to yield more acceptable outputs.

Rarely, if ever, is any attention paid to the
ingredients of the black box itself if its functioning
seems normal. Internal considerations of machine type
black boxes are left to the mechanic, and when repairs
are necessary the unit is no longer functioning as a
black box. If the feedback adjustments are automatic,
as they are in a thermostatic unit, or in a radio's
automatic volume control (AVC) unit, then the unit
can be referred to as cybernetic (that is, its feedback loops are activated automatically according to
some set of previously established criteria for
measuring the unit's outputs).

Consider the black box model of a nuclear
magnetic resonance spectrometer shown in Figure 3.

BLACK BOX
I N P U T S
Magnetic Field
Test Sample
Frequency Setting
Nuclear Magnetic Resonance Spectrometer
Response Curve
Resolution Rate
O U T P U T S
Feedback Loops
(Adjustment in frequency, resolution and magnetic field settings)

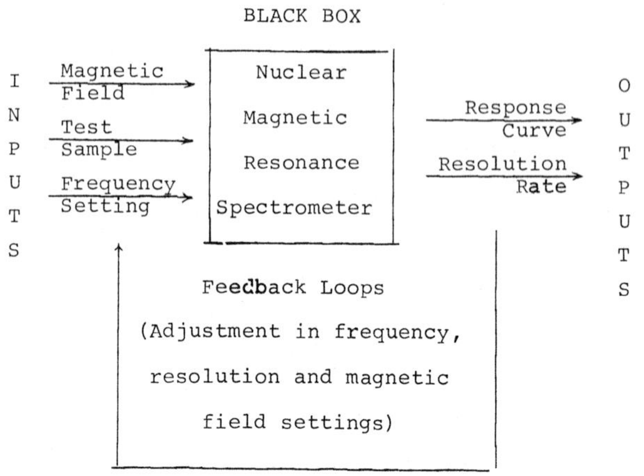

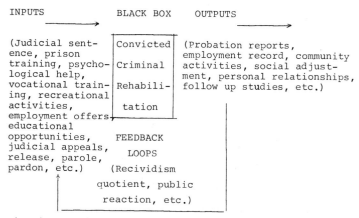

Fig. 3 -- A black box model of a nuclear magnetic resonance spectrometer

INPUTS
BLACK BOX
OUTPUTS
(Judicial sentence, prison training, psychological help, vocational training, recreational activities, employment offers, educational opportunities, judicial appeals, release, parole, pardon, etc.)
Convicted Criminal Rehabilitation
(Probation reports, employment record, community activities, social adjustment, personal relationships, follow up studies, etc.)
FEEDBACK LOOPS
(Recividism quotient, public reaction, etc.)

Fig. 4 -- A black box model for the rehabilitation of a convicted criminal.

Through the use of feedback executed by means of adjustments in wave frequency and magnetic field, the output response pattern can be monitored until the proper output resolution is obtained so as to be able to classify the components of a given test sample input to within the degree of accuracy necessary.

The rehabilitation of a convicted criminal can be viewed as a black box procedure as illustrated in Figure 4.

The black box model is a powerful method of describing relationships in a gross and qualitative manner. Its ability however, to show precise, functional, or quantitative relationships is severely limited. The mere fact that a black box model may have quantitative data attached to its input-output stages does not alter the fact that it is basically a qualitative model form. Figure 5 illustrates the use of typical statistics in the design of a black box model of an average city's use of police resources (inputs), versus the city's crime rates (outputs) as measured by the seven index crimes reported by the F.B.I. each year.[1]

---

1 Consult, J. Edgar Hoover, Uniform Crime Reports for the United States -- 1969 (Washington, D. C.: Government Printing Office, 1970).

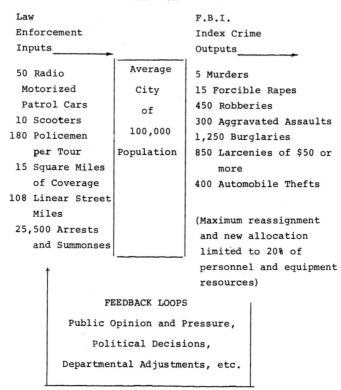

Fig. 5 -- A black box model of an average city's law
enforcement allocations versus its index
crime rates.

In Figure 5, the input-output-feedback data are given numerically, however, the model is still a qualitative one because no functional relationships are presented that can connect or suggest to connect the various criteria in a measurable way. This black box model also is inadequate for quantitative purposes because many outputs such as unreported crimes, white and blue collar crimes, and organized criminal activity are unavoidably omitted. Similarly, a multitude of inputs such as those concerned with social, behavioral, and economic factors also are ignored.

Thus, the black box model of any system can only show the gross connections between some of the input-output-feedback relationships. No claim is made that all of these relationships can ever be shown, or even when they are shown that they can be weighted in accordance with the system and managerial priorities. It is of course, the unknown relationships between the input-output-feedback aspects of any system that make it worth while studying at all. At best, even in the most quantitative OR model, these relationships are only partially modeled. It is primarily for this reason that all OR models must be subjected to constant scrutiny and reevaluation, if they are to be of any value in depicting and predicting reality.

Venn Diagram Models

A Venn diagram is a qualitative model that
represents intersecting subsets of a delineated system.
Its format is a geometrical representation of an all
encompassing set (the Universe), usually depicted by
a rectangle, and the interrelationships of some of
its subsets, depicted by closed curves within the
Universe. However, the relative sizes of the subsets
or their intersections do not necessarily represent
either functional or descriptive relationships.

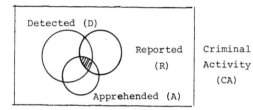

Fig. 6 -- A Venn diagram representing certain
aspects of criminal activity

The Venn diagram illustrated in Figure 6
depicts criminal activity as the Universe, and some
of the relationships among several of its subsets.
For example, the shaded area represents the intersection of three subsets (D $\wedge$ R $\wedge$ A), and indicates
those apprehensions which were both reported and
detected. The area outside the union of the three

subsets {CA - (A ∨ D ∨ R)}, represents those criminal
acts which went undetected, unreported, and unappre-
hended. Appropriate conclusions can be drawn about
other intersected or unioned areas of the illustrated
subsets.

The Venn diagram in Figure 7 can be used to
illustrate a means of evaluating the priority dispatching criteria of law enforcement resources.[1] As
previously noted, no attempt is made to use relative
sizes in order to indicate the proportion of each
type of call.

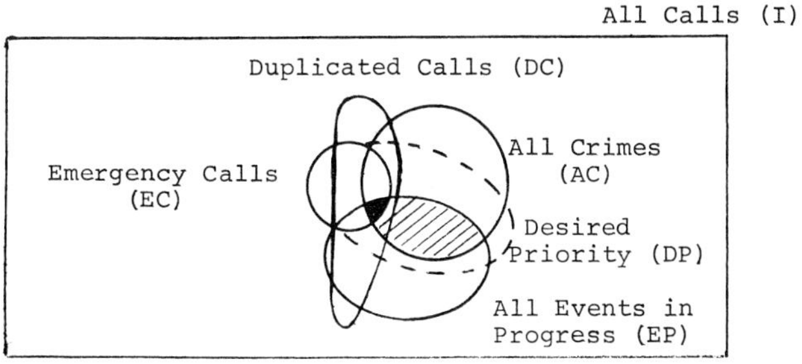

All Calls (I)

Duplicated Calls (DC)

Emergency Calls
(EC)

All Crimes
(AC)

Desired
Priority (DP)

All Events in
Progress (EP)

Fig. 7 -- A Venn diagram depicting priortity
dispatching criteria based on calls
for police service.

---

1 Adapted from, Institute for Defense Analyses, Task
Force Report: Science and Technology (hereinafter
Task Force: SAT), a report to the President's Commission
on Law Enforcement and the Administration of Justice
(Washington, D. C.: Government Printing Office, 1967),
figure B-4, "Priority Dispatching Criteria," 102.

The darkened area (EC ∧ AC ∧ EP), represents those emergency calls which refer to crimes that are in progress. The dotted area represents the desired priority operating region that police dispatchers would like to cover so as to deploy their limited police response resources in an optimal manner. The added variable of keeping track of duplicate telephone calls in reference to the same incident tends to increase the complexity of the police dispatchers' duties, and adds to the problem of seeking an optimal deployment policy.

William W. Herrmann[1] used the elements of Venn diagrams to illustrate the substructures of governmental agencies concerned with CJ, and used the entire government as the Universe. He replaced the Universe (I) used in Venn diagrams with the sociological concept of the Environmental Gestalt (E), but retained all other aspects of Venn diagram modeling. His work also included the novel technique of including a simple flow chart within the Venn diagram to demonstrate the interconnections between the governmental agencies of law enforcement and their objectives,

---

1 William W. Herrmann, "Public Order in a Free Society: A Problem in Suboptimization," in Law Enforcement Science and Technology II: Proceedings of the Second National Symposium on Law Enforcement Science and Technology, ed. by S. I. Cohn (Chicago: IIT Research Institute, 1969), 297-306.

as constrained by social, technological, administrative, political, legal and economic (STAPLE) factors.
Figure 8 is a modification of Herrmann's Venn diagram
model.

Environmental Gestalt (E)

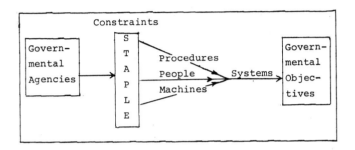

Fig. 8 -- A Venn diagram representing STAPLE constraints
on the objectives of governmental agencies.

The use of Venn diagrams is a convenient way of
illustrating qualitative interrelationships in the CJ
system. The Venn diagram in Figure 9 can be used to
indicate that some automobile thefts are simultaneously
combined with other robberies (A ∧ R), or that some
murders are connected to robberies and automobile
thefts (A ∧ R ∧ M).

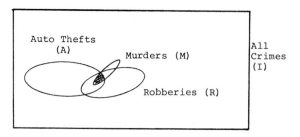

Fig. 9 -- A Venn diagram relating the
interactions of certain crimes.

Baltimore Judicial System (J)

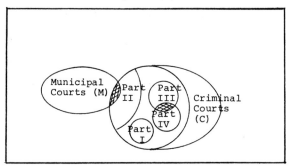

Fig. 10 -- A Venn diagram depicting the arrangement
of the Baltimore Judicial System.

Venn diagrams also can be used to illustrate
extremely involved relationships which would otherwise
require lengthy written explanations. The Venn
diagram in Figure 10, though necessarily incomplete,
nevertheless, shows the major relationships between
the Municipal Court and the five parts of the
Criminal Court system in Baltimore, Maryland. The
information required to make this Venn diagram was
obtained from data supplied by the Institute for
Defense Analyses.[1]

The intersection of Municipal Court cases and
Criminal Court cases (M ∧ C), is handled by Part II
of the Criminal Courts, and they represent appeals
from the Municipal Courts. Part III is the Youth
Court (ages 16 to 21), and its intersection with
Part IV represents those overflow cases from Part
III which are handled in Part IV. Part I cases are
not handled in any other part except by the "catchall
court," Part V which also includes the presentation
of motions.

---

1 Institute for Defense Analyses, Task Force Report:
The Courts, a report to the President's Commission on
Law Enforcement and the Administration of Justice
(Washington, D. C.: U. S. Government Printing Office,
1967), 121-128.

Flow Chart Models

A flow chart is a diagram of specified decision steps (usually binary), which shows the logical sequence of a process or operation from start to finish. It is the most widely used mathematical model in the current CJ literature. Flow charts are principally qualitative modeling devices, but with sufficient adaptation they can be modified to include quantitative data as well. Used in this modified fashion they can be quite informative and descriptive, though rarely predictive.

Flow charts represent a rich and powerful means of modeling processes and operations of the CJ system. The flow chart model can be used to organize procedures, show decision steps, indicate system flows, illustrate executive responsibilities, record dynamic branching processes, and indicate the steps of a computer program. The police interrogation process, and the forensic science evidence evaluation procedure are but two examples of how flow charts can be used to express information quite compactly and effectively.

Probably the most detailed and definitive flow chart of a qualitative nature for the entire CJ system was the one that appeared in Task Force: SAT.[1]

---

1 Task Force: SAT, 58-59.

Decision steps were not labelled in the standard
binary manner, but they were shown in a branching
fashion with the relative thickness of each branch
used to approximate the decreased flow of defendants
at each stage. The flow chart is reproduced in
Figure 11 because a summary of it would not do it
justice.

As a modification of this qualitative flow chart
Task Force: SAT presented a quantified flow chart with
estimated offender flows and direct operating costs
for the United States index crimes of 1965.[1] The
flow chart begins with 2,780,140 reported index crimes,
then proceeds to 727,000 arrests, 177,000 formal felony
complaints, 168,000 trials, 160,000 sentences, and
finally 98,000 imprisonments, at a total estimated
cost of 2.1 billion dollars. The Task Force: SAT
also presented a court flow diagram,[2] a municipal
and county adult corrections flow diagram,[3] and a
State adult corrections flow diagram.[4] In each of

1 Task Force: SAT, Figure 17, "Criminal Justice System
Model with Estimates of Flow of Offenders and Direct
Operating Costs for Index Crimes in the United States
in 1965," 60-61.

2 Ibid., Figure G-4, "Court Flow Diagram," 174-175.

3 Ibid., Figure G-5, "Municipal and County Adult
Corrections Flow Diagram," 176-177.

4 Ibid., Figure G-6, "State Adult Corrections Flow
Diagram," 178-179.

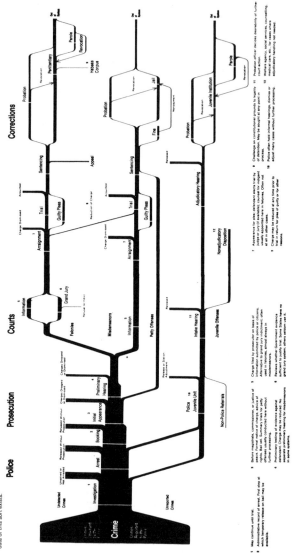

A general view of The Criminal Justice System*

Figure 11

This chart seeks to present a simple yet comprehensive view of the movement of cases through the criminal justice system. Procedures in individual jurisdictions may vary from the pattern shown here. The differing weights of line indicate the relative volumes of cases disposed of at various points in the system, but this is only suggestive since no nationwide data of this sort exists.

* Reduced to 64 per cent of the original size appearing in Task Force: SAT, 58-59.

these cases the flow charts described the typical
operational steps of a defendant moving through the
CJ system in a qualitative manner.

A flow chart with statistical means, numbers of
defendants, 50th, 80th, and 99th percentile figures
for the days between arrest and arraignment steps
in processing of felony defendants, in the District
of Columbia for 1965 was also presented.[1] The total
number of average days from arrest to sentencing for
convicted criminals ranged from a low of 132 to a high
of 216. The total number of average days from arrest
to acquittal ranged from a low of 137 to a high of 213.
Some of the results of that flow chart can be summarized by the black box model in Figure 12.
Circled figures are the recommended number of days by
the Task Force: SAT.

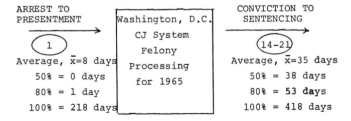

Fig. 12 -- A black box model of felony processing
          in Washington, D. C. for 1965

1 Task Force: SAT, Figure I-2, "Days Between Arrest
and Arraignment Steps in Processing of Felony Defendants -- 1965," 202-203.

The most definitive and quantitative flow chart
of the entire CJ system was presented by Alfred
Blumstein and Richard Larson.[1] The model was linear
and depicted the flow of arrested persons through the
entire CJ system as functions of crime type. By
apportioning costs, establishing probabilistic
recidivisms, and developing crime-switch matrices,
the model served to depict the total costs and
operations of the CJ system, and to project crime rates
based on feedback analyses. Offenders were charted
through the apprehension, adjudication and rehabilitation stages of the CJ system in order to model the
effects of the system on their future criminal behavior.
The study is the most important contribution to the
OR study of the CJ system to date. Because of the
vastness of its undertaking the study was limited to
the analyses of steady-state and linear variables and
consequently its models may be inadequate to describe
the dynamic and non-linear aspects of the CJ system.

The NYSIIS report presented a flow chart of "The
Criminal Justice Process for Adult Felonies."[2]

---

1 Alfred Blumstein and Richard Larson, "Models of a
Total Criminal Justice System," Opns. Res., 17 (March-
April, 1969), 199-232.

2 Dwight C. Smith, Jr., ed., NYSIIS (New York State
Identification and Intelligence System): System
Development Plan, (New York: State Executive Department,
1967), Figure I, nine unnumbered pages in the
"Forward."

The analysis was not as detailed as the one cited
in the Task Force report, but it is qualitatively definitive from the following points of view: the legal
steps to be followed, the forms to be filed, the reports
to be made out, and the general treatment of the
defendant. According to the flow chart, the key
steps to be followed by the CJ system after the
commission of a crime are, in order: arrest, booking,
preliminary arraignment, hearing, grand jury examination, arraignment and plea, trial and verdict, sentence,
probation, incarceration, parole hearing, and freedom.
Some of these steps may of course be bypassed, as
the circumstances permit. Noticeably absent from
the flow chart is a feedback loop for recividism,
especially since the national figure for repeating
offenders is placed around 65 percent.

Philip Ennis[1] showed a flow chart based on interviews with 2,000 crime victims   entitled "Police
Notification and the Judicial Outcome of Victimization." The flow chart in Figure 13 is an expanded
and modified version of the one Ennis presented,
and is designed to follow the procedures used in flow
charts for computer programming. The attrition is
quite obvious, and is typical of the available
national figures on crime victimization. Of the

---

1 Philip H. Ennis, "The Measurement of Crime in the
United States" in Law Enforcement Science and Technology I,
Proceedings of the First National Symposium on Law Enforce-
ment Science and Technology, ed. by S. A. Yefsky (Washington,
D.C.: Thompson Book Co., 1967), 687-693.

original 2,000 victims interviewed, only 25 cases
(or 1.25 per cent of the original 2,000 cases),
resulted in a trial outcome that the victims
thought appropriate.

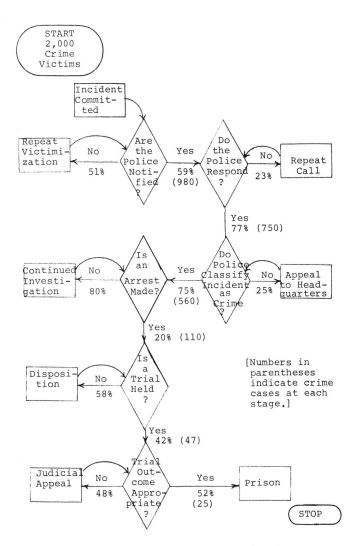

Fig. 13 -- A flow chart of crime victimization:

an examination of police and judicial steps.

CHAPTER VI

THE PROBLEM OF ASSIGNMENT

Administrators in all aspects of the CJ system are constantly faced with the problems of assignment. These problems may take on the form of assigning policemen to precincts, assigning forensic evidence to testing procedures, or assigning sentences to convicted criminals. Despite the fact that the field of CJ provides fertile opportunities for the application of the assignment algorithm, there is no OR or CJ literature that demonstrates how this important method can be so employed.

There are several methods of solving the assignment problem including a demonstration that an $n \times n$ assignment problem is equivalent to a $2n \times n^2$ zero-sum, two person game,[1] or that it is equivalent to an integer programming problem.[2] However, the most widely used procedure is generally

---

[1] John von Neumann, "A Certain Zero-Sum Two-Person Game Equivalent to the Optimal Assignment Problem," in John von Neumann: Collected Works, Vol. VI, ed. by A. H. Taub (New York: The Macmillan Co., 1963), 44-49.

[2] George B. Dantzig, "Discrete-Variable Extremum Problems," Opns. Res., 5 (March-April, 1957), 266-276.

conceded to be the so-called Hungarian method.

The Hungarian method originated with the Hamiltonian Game,[1] and the works of F. Georg Frobenius,[2] Denes König[3] and E. Egerváry,[4] which in turn were refined and applied by H. W. Kuhn.[5] While considering the solution to a related problem known as the "traveling-salesman" problem, Julia Robinson[6] and Merril M. Flood[7] independently contributed valuable results to the present assignment algorithm. The traveling-salesman problem involves finding the minimum route in miles, that a salesman should take in traveling between each of a set of cities during one round trip, based on the known distances between each city-pair. Although special

1 W. W. R. Ball, Mathematical Recreations and Essays, revised by H. S. M. Coxeter, (11th ed.; New York: Macmillan, 1939), 262-266.

2 F. Georg Frobenius, "Uber Matrizen aus Nicht Negativen Elementen," Sitzungsberitche Berliner Akademie 23 (1912), 456-477.

3 Denes König, "Uber Graphen und ihre Anwendung auf Determinatentheorie und Mengenlehre," Mathematische Annalen 77 (1916), 453-465.

4 E. Egerváry, "Matrixok Kombinatorikus Tulajdonsá-gairól," Matematikai es Fizikai Lapok, 38 (1931), 16-28.

5 H. W. Kuhn, "The Hungarian Method for the Assignment Problem," Naval Research Logistics Quarterly 2 (1955), 83-97.

6 Julia Robinson, "On the Hamiltonian Game (A Traveling-Salesman Problem)," RAND Memo RM-303 (Santa Monica, Calif.: RAND Corp., December 5, 1949).

7 Merrill M. Flood, "The Traveling-Salesman Problem," Opns. Res., 4 (January-February, 1956), 61-75.

cases have been solved, the general solution to the traveling-salesman problem is unsolved.

Simply stated, the assignment problem involves the allocation of a set of resources such as men, equipment, material, or tests onto a set of destinations such as jobs, tasks, locations, or machines so as to optimize the assignment, based on known criteria measures such as time, distance, cost, error, or output between the points of resource and destination. A measure matrix, based on a specified criterion, is established that assigns a weight between every resource and destination. The optimization can require either a minimization or a maximization depending on the nature of the criterion used to establish the measure matrix. The assignment is one-to-one, that is, a resource is uniquely assigned to a destination and vice versa.

In order to illustrate the assignment problem, consider the plight of the administrator of a forensic laboratory who has three tasks to assign and exactly three investigators available for assignment. Some possible methods of fulfilling the assignment might be based on drawing lots, playing favorites, having the investigators choose, considering the experience of the investigators at the task, using executive expertise, or appealing to intuition. The method

that follows is designed to discourage the use of
these questionable criteria, and to introduce some
degree of rationality into the method of assignment.

Suppose the administrator, convinced that a
rational procedure should be introduced, decided on
basing the assignment on the average length of time
it takes each investigator to complete each task.
This approach assumes among other things, that the
administrator is convinced that a rational approach
is desirable, that such data is available or can be
collected, and that the completion times to be used
in the measure matrix represent average values each
derived from data with small statistical variance.

Consider the following measure matrix M, based
on the criterion of completion times (c_{ij}), where
for example, entry C_{23} or $(2,3)$ indicates that it
takes investigator B 8 minutes, on the average, to
complete task III. If average values, or some other
suitable statistical measures are unavailable, then
best estimated times may be used so long as their
associated degrees of uncertainty are taken into
consideration.

$$
\begin{array}{c}
 & \begin{array}{ccc} \text{I} & \text{II} & \text{III} \end{array} \\
\begin{array}{c} \text{A} \\ \text{B} \\ \text{C} \end{array} &
\left(\begin{array}{ccc}
② & 6 & 3 \\
5 & ① & 8 \\
5 & 7 & ④
\end{array}\right)
\end{array}
\qquad \text{Measure Matrix M}
$$

The objective of this allocation is to minimize the total completion time for the three tasks, so that the optimal solution in this case will be the one that minimizes the total one-to-one assignment. The circles indicate the task time that is minimum for each investigator, and in this case, this suboptimization is also the overall optimal assignment. Such fortunately obvious solutions rarely befall administrators however, so a more systematic assignment method will now be outlined.

The first impulse might be to use the trial and error method of solving the assignment problem by enumerating all of the possible ordered triples. In an n × n assignment problem, there are n^2 measures or weights that must be assigned as a means of relating each source to every destination. Since the first choice can be made in n ways, the second in n-1 ways, etc., there are in general n! possible assignments. In this case the six ways $(3! = 3 \cdot 2 \cdot 1 = 6)$, are tabulated along with their total completion times in Table 1. Assignment 1 would be the first choice, assignment 6 the second choice, up to assignment 4 as the last choice, when the optimal solution requires a minimization of total completion time. However, if the measure matrix measured units of output per unit

TABLE 1

ENUMERATED POSSIBILITIES FOR A 3 × 3

ASSIGNMENT PROBLEM IN FORENSIC SCIENCE

Investigators	Possible Assignments					
	1	2	3	4	5	6
A	I	I	II	II	III	III
B	II	III	I	III	I	II
C	III	II	III	I	II	I
Total Completion Times of Assignments in Minutes	7	17	15	19	15	9

time rather than completion times, the optimal solution would require a maximization, and thus, the preceding choices would be reversed.

In order to evaluate just how inefficient the method of complete enumeration actually is, consider the relatively small executive problem of assigning 48 men to 48 jobs. There are 48! or about 12.4×10^{60} possibilities to consider. If each of one trillion (10^{12}) computers tested a trillion assignments every second, then it would take more than 10^{29} years to test all the possible assignments. Since the age of the Earth is generally placed at only 10^{13} years, it is immediately obvious that even the most sophisticated computer technology would not be

sufficient to make the trial and error procedure
a feasible method of solution for the n × n assignment problem.

A modified and expanded form of the Hungarian
method of solving the assignment problem will now
be outlined.[1] The basic steps may be summarized as
follows if the optimization requires a minimization
of the measure matrix M.

1. Select the lowest value in each row of matrix M
of order n and subtract this value from each entry
in that row to form a new matrix M'.

2. Select the lowest value in each column of matrix
M' and subtract this value from each entry in that
column to form a new matrix M".

3. The first two steps will produce at least n zeroes
in matrix M". Steps 1. and 2. can be reversed due
to duality without affecting the succeeding steps,
but the M" matrices so obtained will not generally
be the same.

4. Determine the minimum number of covering lines
(L_{min}), that can be drawn through all the zeros
of matrix M" along its rows and columns. If $L_{min} = n$,

1 Consult, David W. Miller and Martin K. Starr,
Executive Decisions and Operations Research (2nd.
ed.; Englewood Cliffs, N. J.: Prentice-Hall, 1969),
247-260.

then by the König-Egerváry theorem, matrix M" contains
at least one optimal solution, which can be determined
by step 10.

5. If there is any row or column without a zero, then
proceed to step 8. since it is obvious that $L_{min} < n$.
It is also obvious that in any n × n matrix, n lines
will also be sufficient to cover all the zeros
-- the difficulty lies in finding L_{min}.

6. When it is not clear how to determine L_{min}, as
is often the case, the following procedure can be
employed:[1]

   a) Locate any row that has only one zero, box that
      position and then cross out any zeros
      appearing in its corresponding column.

   b) Repeat a) for the columns, and continue until
      all zero positions have been boxed or crossed out.

   c) If the boxed positions comprise a complete
      one-to-one assignment then proceed to step 10;
      if not, then proceed to step 7.

7. L_{min} can now be determined by the following procedure:

   a) Star each row that does not have a boxed position.

   b) Star each column which contains a zero(s) in a
      starred row.

1 Consult, Frederick S. Hillier and Gerald J. Lieberman,
Introduction to Operations Research (San Francisco:
Holden-Day, Inc., 1968), 201-204.

c) Star each row that has a boxed position in a starred column.

d) L_{min} is the set of lines drawn through each unstarred row, and through each starred column.

8. If $L_{min} < n$, then select the smallest weight of matrix M" that is not covered by a line. Subtract that value from all the uncovered weights in matrix M", and add that value to any weights that may be covered by two intersecting lines in matrix M", so as to form a transformed matrix M^{*}.

9. Repeat steps 6. through 8. until the condition that $L_{min} = n$ is satisfied by some transformed matrix M^{**}.

10. When $L_{min} = n$, the locations of the zeros in matrix M" or M^{**} specify the feasible positions for the optimal assignment. If more than one feasible zero is available in any row or column of matrix M" or M^{**}, then the optimal assignment may not be unique. Contrary to certain mathematical conditions of uniqueness, such options are welcomed by executives since they represent alternative optimal allocations with the same total costs, and thus provide a degree of flexibility in making the overall assignment. The optimal alternatives are determined by tabulating the zero positions for each row, and then testing

the feasibility of each combination of assignments in a manner similar to step 6.

Applying the first two steps of the assignment algorithm to the example yields:

$$M = \begin{pmatrix} 2 & 6 & 3 \\ 5 & 1 & 8 \\ 5 & 7 & 4 \end{pmatrix} \xrightarrow{\text{Use Step 1.}} M' = \begin{pmatrix} 0 & 4 & 1 \\ 4 & 0 & 7 \\ 1 & 3 & 0 \end{pmatrix} \xrightarrow{\text{Use Step 2.}} M'' = \begin{pmatrix} 0 & 4 & 1 \\ 4 & 0 & 7 \\ 1 & 3 & 0 \end{pmatrix}$$

The zeros of matrix M'' can be covered by no fewer than three lines, in more than the following two ways:

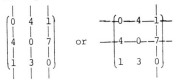

Thus, in this case steps 6. through 9. are unnecessary since $L_{min} = n$. An application of step 10. confirms that the optimal solution obtained previously was unique. Thus, the assignment of A → I, B → II, and C → III is minimal, with a total overall completion time of 7 minutes.

Suppose however, that the original matrix M was transformed by a reversal of entries c_{21} and c_{22} so as to form matrix N, then the solution would proceed as follows:

$$N = \begin{pmatrix} 2 & 6 & 3 \\ 1 & 5 & 8 \\ 5 & 7 & 4 \end{pmatrix} \xrightarrow[\text{Step}]{\text{Use}} N' = \begin{pmatrix} 0 & 4 & 1 \\ 0 & 4 & 7 \\ 1 & 3 & 0 \end{pmatrix} \xrightarrow[\text{Step}]{\text{Use}} N'' = \begin{pmatrix} 0 & 1 & 1 \\ 0 & 1 & 7 \\ 1 & 0 & 0 \end{pmatrix}$$

Applying step 6. to matrix N" yields, for example:

$$\begin{pmatrix} \boxed{0} & 1 & 1 \\ \emptyset & 1 & 7 \\ 1 & \boxed{0} & \emptyset \end{pmatrix}$$

The assignment is incomplete so that it is necessary to proceed to step 7.:

In this case only the two indicated lines are necessary to cover all the zeros of matrix N". Thus, $L_{min} < n$ (2 < 3), and the algorithm solution proceeds to step 8. as follows:

In Matrix N^*, no fewer than three lines can be used to cover all the zeros, so the algorithm solution

proceeds to step 10. This time however, there is
a degree of flexibility in the overall assignment.
A determination of the equivalent assignments can
be made by tabulating the potential assignments for
each investigator (according to the locations of
zeros in matrix N^*), specifying a feasible task
(by using a circle), and then by successively striking
out any duplication in assignment for the other
investigators as follows, with the results summarized
in Table 2:

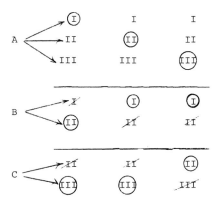

TABLE 2

OPTIMAL ALTERNATIVE SOLUTIONS WITH MINIMUM

TIMES INDICATED FOR A 3 × 3 ASSIGNMENT PROBLEM

Alternative Assignments	Optimal Allocations	Time in Minutes for Each Assignment
1	A-I, B-II, C-III	2+5+4 = 11
2	A-II, B-I , C-III	6+1+4 = 11
3	A-III, B-I, C-II	3+1+7 = 11

Each of the three optimal assignments has a
total minimum time value of 11 minutes. It should
be noted that unlike the original problem in which
the administrator was able to assign each investigator to his most efficient task (at least in terms
of the completion time criterion), in this case the
optimal solutions depended on the more typical situation which required trade-off considerations. For
example, in alternative assignment 3, A is assigned
to his second fastest task, III (3 minutes), and
C is assigned to his slowest task, II (7 minutes),
while only B is assigned to his fastest task, I
(1 minute). Thus, while all three assignments have

the same total minimum time, assignment 1 utilizes
"two first and a second," assignment 2 utilizes
"two firsts and a third," and assignment 3 utilizes
"one first, one second and one third." The administrator can now apply his own expertise, and consider
other unmeasurable factors in deciding which of
these optimal solutions to implement.

Even before implementing an optimal unique
assignment such as the one previously derived for
matrix M, the administrator may correctly wish to
apply other criteria in addition to that of total
task completion time. For example, the administrator
may very well want to consider criteria such as the
quality of the work, the cost of the assignment,
the preferences of the investigators, and the amount
of additional training required. Certainly, a suitable
measure matrix can be established for each of these
criteria, and any others that might be considered.
However, since assignments based on diverse criteria
will be generally from different measure matrices,
how will the administrator resolve the resulting
contradictions, especially when the measuring scales
that might be employed such as time, distance, output,
and quantity may not be compatible?

One method of utilizing the various criteria to
form a single measure matrix is to assign utilities

to each criterion,[1] and then to establish an
optimal assignment based on a single weighted measure
matrix. The principle of employing a weighted
measure matrix derived from a consideration of
utilities is theoretically sound, but its use
requires overcoming several practical difficulties,
such as the assumption that the various criteria can
be given values from a uniform utility scale. In
general, this is no mean task, and in some instances
it is just impossible to carry out.

To illustrate a method of solving the assignment
problem based on more than one criterion, consider
the following three matrices considered by the forensic
science administrator in an attempt to determine an
optimal assignment based on additional considerations.
In each case, the measurement criterion has been
converted to time in minutes over one tour of duty.
Thus, in matrix Q, the quality of work criterion as
represented by the number of average errors, is
measured by the additional time in minutes needed
to correct errors, rather than being measured by
the average number of errors. The additional training
time criterion required by the investigators for

---

1 Consult, Stephen S. Willoughby, "Representations
by Means of Formal Mathematical Structures," (unpublished Ed.D. dissertation, Columbia University, 1961),
22-65, for more details on utility theory and its
applications.

an unfamiliar task, as represented by the average additional time for completing each task, is measured in necessary additional completion time in minutes by matrix T.

The assignment preference criterion of the investigators is converted to its dual consideration and is called the complaint index or criterion. The dual of the preference criterion (complaint) is considered in this case so as to be consistent with the objective of optimization through minimization. Since preference measures would require a maximization, using the dual avoids the complexity of dealing with mixed objectives. This complaint index is measured by matrix C as the additional estimated time in minutes that is added to the completion time of each task due to an investigator's dissatisfaction with an assignment. For this example, the completion time entries in matrix M are considered as ideal least values under the relatively perfect conditions of no performed errors, no added training required, and no assignment dissatisfaction.

$$M=\begin{pmatrix} ⓛ & 6 & 3 \\ 5 & ① & 8 \\ 5 & 7 & ④ \end{pmatrix} \quad Q=\begin{pmatrix} ② & 3 & 1 \\ 4 & 3 & ① \\ 3 & ② & 1 \end{pmatrix} \quad T=\begin{pmatrix} 9 & ③ & 2 \\ 6 & 4 & ② \\ ① & 5 & 7 \end{pmatrix} \quad C=\begin{pmatrix} 4 & 9 & ① \\ ① & 2 & 7 \\ 3 & ③ & 8 \end{pmatrix}$$

Minimum Time = 7 minutes	Minimum Time = 5 minutes	Minimum Time = 6 minutes	Minimum Time = 5 minutes

All entries in the matrices above are in
minutes, and as with matrix M, the objective is to
minimize the overall assignment in each case.
Because of the small number of possible assignments
(only six in each case), it is not difficult to
obtain the overall minimum assignment in each case
without resorting to the use of the algorithm.
The optimal assignments turn out to be different
for each of the four criteria employed, and are
summarized in Table 3.

TABLE 3

OPTIMAL ASSIGNMENT OF FORENSIC SCIENCE

INVESTIGATORS BASED ON FOUR DIFFERENT CRITERIA

Investi-gators	Measure Matrix Criteria			
	Task-Time (M)	Error-Time (Q)	Training-Time (T)	Complaint-Time (C)
A	I	I	II	III
B	II	III	III	I
C	III	II	I	II
Total Completion Times of Assignments in Minutes	7	5	6	5

Since there is no confirmation in assignments
among any of the four criteria measures, the administrator is faced with the problem of sorting through
four different results in order to reach an overall
assignment that somehow considers all of them. As
previously mentioned, one method of resolving this
difficulty would be to establish utilities for each
criteria. There is currently, no purely rational
method for assigning such utilities, and one present
practice is to have the administrator devise utilities
based on his subjective personal expertise, experience, and preference.[1]

Suppose that as a first attempt at determining
a combined optimal assignment, each criterion is
weighted equally. Taking 1/4 of each matrix entry
value, the weighted total matrix W is obtained such
that each entry is the sum of the corresponding
entries of each matrix.

$$W_{ij} = \frac{1}{4} (M_{ij} + Q_{ij} + T_{ij} + C_{ij})$$

$$W = \frac{1}{4} \begin{bmatrix} 17 & 21 & \boxed{7} \\ 16 & \boxed{10} & 18 \\ \boxed{12} & 17 & 20 \end{bmatrix}$$

---

1 Consult, Howard Raiffa, Decision Analysis, (Reading,
Mass.: Addison-Wesley Publishing Co., 1968), 104-128,
for more details on making subjective choices under uncertain conditions.

This weighted matrix W can itself be subjected to the assignment algorithm, which yields the optimal solution of A → III, B → II, C → I, with a total minimum time of 29/4 minutes. This optimal assignment is again different from the previous four, but has the distinctive merit of being the result of considering the combined weighted effects of all four criteria.

The utilities (u_i) associated with the four criteria can be assigned in any proportion, as long as the normalizing consideration, $\sum_{i=1}^{n} u_i = 1$, is applied. That is, the sum of the n utilities imposed (in this case n = 4), must be equal to one. The condition $\sum_{i=1}^{n} u_i = 1$, is used for convenience, and merely represents the decimal equivalents of the assigned utilities considered as percentages of importance or emphasis. For example, an administrator may wish to use the following distribution of utilities: completion time 30% or .3, quality of work 40% or .4, training time 10% or .1, and personnel preference 20% or .2. In this case, the measure matrix W' is generated by: W' = .3M + .4Q + .1T + .2C, and coincidently yields the same optimal assignment.

$$W' = \begin{pmatrix} 3.1 & 5.1 & \boxed{1.7} \\ 4.3 & \boxed{2.3} & 4.4 \\ \boxed{3.4} & 4.0 & 3.9 \end{pmatrix}$$

In general, a combined criteria measure matrix derived from weighted utilities can be generated by: $W = u_1C_1 + u_2C_2 + \ldots + u_iC_i + \ldots + u_nC_n$, where u_i is the assigned utility weight and C_i is the particular measure matrix of a specified criterion.

So far the optimal assignments have only been concerned with minimization. If a measure matrix is derived from a criterion that is to be maximized such as output, efficiency, accuracy, or profit, the algorithm previously developed requires the addition of just one step before proceeding to step 1. The measure matrix is converted from one which requires maximization to one which requires the dual consideration of minimization. This complementation is accomplished by subtracting all matrix entries (m_{ij}) from some suitably high value (S), so that $(S - m_{ij}) \geq 0$. This positive requirement is one of convenience only. It assures that the transformation matrix $\bar{M}$ will contain only positive entries. However, the algorithm would work equally well if all the entries (m_{ij}) were assigned a negative sign.

In order to illustrate this principle, consider that the total assignment based on the original matrix M was to be maximized rather than minimized. The solution based on units of output per unit of time for example, would proceed as follows:

$$M = \begin{pmatrix} 2 & 6 & 3 \\ 5 & 1 & 8 \\ 5 & 7 & 4 \end{pmatrix} \quad \bar{M} = \begin{pmatrix} 10-2 & 10-6 & 10-3 \\ 10-5 & 10-1 & 10-8 \\ 10-5 & 10-7 & 10-4 \end{pmatrix} = \begin{pmatrix} 8 & 4 & 7 \\ 5 & 9 & 2 \\ 5 & 3 & 6 \end{pmatrix}$$

$$\bar{M} \xrightarrow[\text{1.}]{\text{Use} \atop \text{Step}} \begin{pmatrix} 4 & 0 & 3 \\ 3 & 7 & 0 \\ 2 & 0 & 3 \end{pmatrix} \xrightarrow[\text{2.}]{\text{Use} \atop \text{Step}} \begin{pmatrix} 2 & 0 & 3 \\ 1 & 7 & 0 \\ 0 & 0 & 3 \end{pmatrix} \xrightarrow[\text{6.}]{\text{Use} \atop \text{Step}} \begin{pmatrix} 2 & \boxed{0} & 3 \\ 1 & 7 & \boxed{0} \\ \boxed{0} & \emptyset & 3 \end{pmatrix}$$

The value of 10 was selected arbitrarily, 100, 8, or 22.6 would have served as well. The new matrix $\bar{M}$ is now the dual of matrix M with a reversal of high and low values. Now the minimization principles as previously discussed, can be applied to matrix $\bar{M}$. The optimal assignment A → II, B → III, C → I, is unique, and the overall optimal value is 19 output units (or 11 "units" in $\bar{M}$, the dual-min value).

CHAPTER VII

THE PROBLEM OF TRANSPORTATION

The problem of assignment, discussed in Chapter VI is considered to be a special case of the transportation problem which in turn is classified as a linear programming problem. Whereas the assignment problem deals with one-to-one allocations, the transportation problem deals with the transfer of quantities of supplies (s_i), such as men, equipment, or material from sources (m_i), to potential destinations (n_j), such as jobs, locations or machines, which have their own associated demands (d_j).

The measurement criteria weights (c_{ij}), such as time, distance, cost, and output, are assumed known for all mn possible transfers from m sources to n destinations. As with the assignment problem, criteria weights are either taken herein as average measured values or best estimated values, with no attempt made to account for statistical variance or stochastic considerations. It is assumed that

$\sum_{i=1}^{m} s_i = \sum_{j=1}^{n} d_j$, that is, supply equals demand. When
this condition of equality is not met, the problem
is balanced by adding dummy sources or destinations
as needed, so that excess supply is stored at zero
cost, or excess demand is unfilled at infinite cost.
The transportation problem can now be described as
the attempt to find that allocation of supplies to
demands (x_{ij}), over the criteria weights (c_{ij}),
that satisfies the problem constraints in optimal
fashion. It is always possible to find an optimal
solution to the transportation problem when s_i and
d_j are integers, as well as for certain other real
values of s_i and d_j.

The transportation problem, also known as the
Hitchcock-Koopmans transportation problem, generally
is considered to have been formulated first by
Frank L. Hitchcock,[1] and independently later by
L. Kantorovitch,[2] and Tjalling C. Koopmans.[3] There
are several methods of solving the transportation

1 Frank L. Hitchcock, "The Distribution of a Product
from Several Sources to Numerous Localities," Journal
of Mathematics and Physics, 20 (1941), 224-230.

2 L. Kantorovitch, "On the Translocation of Masses,"
Management Science, 5 (October, 1958), 1-4.

3 Tjalling C. Koopmans, "Optimum Utilization of the
Transportation System," Econometrica, 17, supplement
(1949), 136-146.

problem. These include, the simplex technique employed by George B. Dantzig,[1] the stepping-stone method of A. Charnes and W. W. Cooper,[2] the network flow procedures of L. R. Ford and D. R. Fulkerson,[3] and the computational approach of Alex Orden.[4]

As with the assignment problem, there is no application of transportation problem techniques to similar problems that arise in activities of the CJ system, in either the OR or CJ literature. Potential applications include, the temporary reallocation of units of police personnel from available sources to contingency demand locations, the allocation of batches of evaluated evidence to storage points while awaiting court trial demands, and the redistribution of prisoners from overcrowded institutions to those that are under utilized.

Consider the problem of the corrections administrator who wants to transfer prisoners from two

1 George B. Dantzig, "Application of the Simples Method to a Transportation Problem," in Activity Analysis of Production and Allocation, T. C. Koopmans ed., (New York: John Wiley & Sons, Inc., 1951), 359-373.

2 A. Charnes and W. W. Cooper, "The Stepping Stone Method of Explaining Linear Programming Calculations in Transportation Problems," Management Science, 1 (October, 1954), 46-69.

3 L. R. Ford and D. R. Fulkerson, "Solving the Transportation Problem," Management Science, 3 (October, 1956), 24-32.

4 Alex Orden, "The Transhipment Problem," Management Science, 2 (April, 1956), 276-285.

overcrowded jails (sources A and B), to two under-
utilized jails (destinations I and II). Assume that
the overcrowding at A is 50 prisoners and that at B
it is 20 prisoners, also that the under utilization
at I is 40 convict-spaces and that at II it is 30
convict-spaces. How can the transfer be effected in
an optimal manner? It should be noted that the
allocation is a balanced one -- the "supply" of 70
prisoners from A and B, equals the "demand" for 70
prisoners from I and II.

 The corrections administrator must first decide
upon a criterion for the measure matrix which is to
be used to establish an optimal transfer policy.
Assume that it is decided to use the criterion based
on the average cost of transfer per inmate between
the sources and the destinations. Assume also, that
these costs are known, and are given in hundreds of
dollars by the following measure matrix.

TABLE 4

A TRANSPORTATION PROBLEM FOR THE OPTIMAL
TRANSFER OF PRISONERS FROM OVERCROWDED TO
UNDER UTILIZED INSTITUTIONS

		40	30	Demand
Supply	Source	I	II	Destination
50	A	5	3	
20	B	6	2	

For example, it costs three hundred dollars to transfer one inmate from prison A to prison II. Since the objective in this case is to establish an optimal transfer policy for inmates with least overall cost, the transportation problem solution requires a minimization of total cost.

Unlike the assignment problem, which in this case would involve choosing one of two alternatives, there are 21 possible transfer policies in this 2 × 2 transportation problem. Thus, any completely enumerative method for finding the optimal solution to the transportation problem is clearly more inefficient than it was proven to be for the assignment problem. The literature does not indicate any method for determining the total number of possible integer allocations that satisfy the conditions of a given transportation problem because most of them are not feasible solutions. However, the number of possible allocations (P) is generally quite high, and it is conjectured to be represented by the following inequality:

$$P[T_{mn}(s_i, d_j)] \leq$$
$$(m-1)(n-1)\{Max(m-1, n-1)\}\{Min(\min s_i+1, \min d_j+1)\}.$$

In this case, the number of possible allocations, would be given as follows:

$$P \leq (2-1)(2-1) \, Max(1,1) \, Min(21, 31)$$
$$P \leq (1)(1)(1)(21) = 21 .$$

Suppose an arbitrary allocation is made as
follows:

$$
\begin{array}{cc}
40 & 30 \\
\text{I} & \text{II}
\end{array}
$$

$$
\begin{array}{cc}
50 & A \\
20 & B
\end{array}
\left(
\begin{array}{cc}
5^{50} & 3^{0} \\
6^{0} & 2^{20}
\end{array}
\right)
$$

Clearly this cannot be a feasible solution because
50 inmates were assigned to prison I which can only
house 40, and only 20 were assigned to prison II
which can house 30. Any feasible transportation
solution must satisfy the constraints and limitations
set by the problem, and this first trial has not.
By using iterative procedures, 10 inmates can be
transferred from I to II, at a saving of two hundred
dollars per transfer, so as to form the following
transfer policy.

$$
\begin{array}{cc}
40 & 30 \\
\text{I} & \text{II}
\end{array}
$$

$$
\begin{array}{cc}
50 & A \\
20 & B
\end{array}
\left(
\begin{array}{cc}
5^{40} & 3^{10} \\
6^{0} & 2^{20}
\end{array}
\right)
$$

This last allocation is a **feasible** solution since
all the constraints have been met, and the sums of
all the inmate allocations correspond to the supply
and demand specifications. That is, 40+10=50,
0+20=20, 40+0=40, and 10+20=30. However, does this

solution represent the optimal allocation that provides for total minimum cost?

The optimal solution to this problem will be found now by iterative considerations. Any transfer from (A,I) to (A,II) would decrease costs by two hundred dollars per inmate, but in order to maintain the constraint of 30 units of demand an equal number of inmates from (B,II) would have to be transferred to (B,I) at an increased cost of four hundred dollars per inmate. The net increased cost is two hundred dollars per inmate transferred. Thus, this iteration policy would result in an increased total cost for the inmate transfers. By similar iterative considerations, it can be shown that the above allocation is indeed optimal, and has a total minimal cost of $5 \cdot 40 + 3 \cdot 10 + 6 \cdot 0 + 2 \cdot 20 = 270$ hundred dollars. All of the other twenty allocations are of higher total cost:

$$\begin{pmatrix} 5^{20} & 3^{30} \\ 6^{20} & 2^{0} \end{pmatrix}, \begin{pmatrix} 5^{21} & 3^{29} \\ 6^{19} & 2^{1} \end{pmatrix}, \begin{pmatrix} 5^{22} & 3^{28} \\ 6^{18} & 2^{2} \end{pmatrix}, \cdots \begin{pmatrix} 5^{39} & 3^{11} \\ 6^{1} & 2^{19} \end{pmatrix}$$

Cost=310, Cost=308, Cost=306,... Cost=272

Unlike the assignment problem, there is no need for the transportation matrix to be square (n × n). Consider an extension of the correction administrator's problem to include another overcrowded prison C with $s_3 = 30$, with the same number of under utilized jails

(n=2), but with demand totals readjusted to 100 in
order to balance the supply from jails A, B, and C.

$$
\begin{array}{cc}
& 40 \quad 60 \\
& \text{I} \quad \text{II} \\
\begin{array}{cc}50 & A \\ 20 & B \\ 30 & C\end{array} &
\left(\begin{array}{cc} 5 & 3 \\ 6 & 2 \\ 1 & 8 \end{array}\right)
\end{array}
$$

As in the previous case, the optimal allocation
will require a minimization of the total cost. This
time however, for purposes of illustration, the
measure criterion will be expressed in terms of
average prison guard hours per inmate required to
effect the transfers. Undoubtedly, the previous
criterion and the present one are not entirely
independent. However, both require different formulations, the former is primarily budgetary, while the
latter is primarily concerned with the use of personnel.
Identical entries are used in the first two rows of
the new transportation problem only as a matter of
convenience, and it should be noted that normally they
would be quite different.

It has been shown that in an m × n transportation
matrix, the optimal solution requires no more than
(m + n - 1) nonzero allocations. Since there are a
total of mn allocations, the dual statement is that

in an optimal solution there must be at least
(mn-m-n+1) zero allocations. A feasible solution
that meets the additional condition of exactly
(m+n-1) nonzero allocations is known as a basic
feasible solution. A degenerate solution is one
in which the optimal allocation contains less than
(m+n-1) nonzero allocations. For example, the
following optimal minimum cost solution contains only
three nonzero allocations, whereas (m+n-1) equals
four. Thus, the transportation solution, though
valid and optimal, would be referred to as degenerate.

$$
\begin{array}{cc}
30 & 70
\end{array}
$$

$$
\begin{array}{c}
50 \\
20 \\
30
\end{array}
\left(
\begin{array}{cc}
5 & 3^{50} \\
6 & 2^{20} \\
1^{30} & 8
\end{array}
\right)
$$

The following algorithm represents a modification
and an expansion of the method developed by William
R. Vogel[1] which generally is considered to be the most
efficient hand method for solving the transportation
problem. Although the method is referred to as an
algorithm, there are occasionally, several iterations

1 Consult, "VAM -- Vogel's Approximation Method," in
Nyles V. Reinfeld and William R. Vogel, Mathematical
Programming (Englewood Cliffs, N. J.; Prentice-Hall,
Inc., 1960), 59-70.

required before an optimal solution is obtained.
It should be noted, that the widely used "Northwest
Passage" initial allocation procedure, although it
assures (m+n-1) nonzero allocations, invariably leads
to a high initial cost allocation when minimizing,
and thus inefficiently requires many lengthy iterations
before the optimal solution can be obtained.

Step 1. If the optimal solution requires a maximization, select the highest c_{ij} in matrix C, call it c'_{ij},
and subtract all other c_{ij} values from it, that is
$(c'_{ij} - c_{ij})$, so as to form a complementary matrix $\bar{C}$,
and then proceed to step 2. This procedure guarantees
that the entries of matrix $\bar{C}$ will be positive, and is
merely a matter of convenience. The same effect can
be established by negating each entry of matrix C.
If the optimal solution requires a minimization,
then proceed to step 2 directly.

Step 2. Form a new tabulation that has an additional
column made up of minimum differences (c_i), between
the lowest c_{ij} value in each row and the next lowest
c_{ij} value in that row, and an additional row made up
of minimum differences (c_j), between the lowest c_{ij}
value in each column and the next lowest c_{ij} value
in that column. For the previously cited example,
this new tabulation follows:

	40	60	c_i
50	5	3	2
20	6	2	4
30	1	8	7
c_j	4	1	

Step 3. Select the largest value from among the c_i and c_j differences, and allocate to the lowest c_{ij} in that row or column the total remaining supply or the total remaining demand value, whichever is least. Ties between c_i or c_j values can be broken by considering the highest second differences. Continuing with the same example, this step is executed as follows:

	40	60	c_i
50	5	3	2
20	6	2	4
30	1^{30}	8	7
c_j	4	1	

Step 4. The row or column which has been allocated an entire supply or demand, as explained in step 3., now is omitted from consideration, and steps 2. and 3. are repeated. For the same example, this yields:

	40	60	c_i			40	60	c_i
50	5	3	2		50	5	3	2
Step 2. → 20	6	2	4	Step 3. → 20	6	2^{20}	4
30	1^{30}	8	−		30	1^{30}	8	−
c_j	1	1		c_j	1	1	

Step 5. Repeat step 4. until all supply and demand values are allocated. This method assures that there will be $(m+n-1)$ nonzero allocations, unless a row and a column are simultaneously eliminated by the appliation of step 3., in which case the feasible solution will be degenerate as previously explained. The last allocation of 10 units to the c_{11} position is mandatory.

	40	60	c_i			40	60	c_i
50	5	3	2		50	5^{10}	3^{40}	2
Step 2. → 20	6	2^{20}	−	Step 3. → 20	6	2^{20}	−
30	1^{30}	8	−		30	1^{30}	8	−
c_j	1	5		c_j	1	5	

Step 6. In order to test the optimality of the allocation obtained through an application of the first five steps, a test matrix C^* is formed such that, $c^*_{ij} = u_i + v_j$. The row values u_i, and the column values v_j are obtained arbitrarily by letting $u_1 = 0$, and then solving the $(m+n-1)$ independent equations involving the u_i, v_j, and c_{ij} values that

have received an allocation. For the example
discussed this becomes:

$$
\begin{array}{cc}
 & u_i \\
\begin{pmatrix} 5^{10} & 3^{40} \\ 6 & 2^{20} \\ 1^{30} & 8 \end{pmatrix} & \begin{matrix} 0 \\ -1 \\ -4 \end{matrix}
\end{array}
\qquad
\begin{array}{lll}
u_1+v_1= 5 & \text{Let } u_1=0, & \text{then } v_1=5. \\
u_1+v_2= 3 & \text{But } u_1=0, \text{ so} & v_2=3. \\
u_2+v_2= 2 & \text{But } v_2=3, \text{ so} & u_2=-1. \\
u_3+v_1= 1 & \text{But } v_1=5, \text{ so} & u_3=-4.
\end{array}
$$

$$v_j \qquad 5 \qquad 3$$

$$
c^* = c^*_{ij} = (u_i+v_j) = \begin{pmatrix} 5 & 3 \\ 4 & 2 \\ 1 & -1 \end{pmatrix}
$$

Step 7. If all the entries of the test matrix c^*
satisfy the condition $c^*_{ij} \leq c_{ij}$, then the original
allocation is optimal. The c^*_{ij} values that correspond
to nonzero allocation positions must of course, have
the same value as their corresponding entries in the
original matrix C. However, if there are other
values such that $c^*_{ij} = c_{ij}$, then the positions for
which this occurs represent potential locations to
which the supply and demand figures can be reassigned
in order to yield the alternate optimal solutions
with the same total cost. In the illustrated example,
the allocation was optimal since $c^*_{ij} \leq c_{ij}$.

Step 8. If there are entries in the test matrix
such that $c_{ij}^* > c_{ij}$, then the original solution is
not optimal. In order to obtain the optimal solution,
the highest ($c_{ij}^* - c_{ij}$) entry is selected, and the
largest reallocation of resources possible is assigned
to that position. This reallocation process is an
iterative one, and the decisions for it are made by
considering net effects of resource transfers around
a closed subset of the c_{ij} entries.

Step 9. If step 8. is necessary, then repeat step 6.
until the conditions of step 7. are met. The allocation will then be optimal, and the total cost of the
transportation can be computed by taking the sum of
the products of the units allocated to the positions
of cost per unit transport. That is, optimization of
$\{ \sum_{i=1}^{m} \sum_{j=1}^{n} x_{ij} c_{ij} \}$. For the illustrated example this
becomes:

Total Transportation Cost =

(10)(5) + (40)(3) + (0)(6) + (20)(2) + (30)(1)+ (0)(8)

= 50 + 120 + 0 + 40 + 30 + 0

= 240 prison-guard hours.

It is not unusual for the initial basic feasible
solution obtained by this algorithm to be optimal, as
it was in the previous example. For the purposes of
comparison, the Northwest Passage procedure for

obtaining an initial basic feasible solution to the
transportation problem is sketched below.

$$
\begin{array}{c}
\cancel{30} \\
\cancel{50} \\
\cancel{40}\cancel{60} \\
\cancel{10}\cancel{50}\left(\begin{array}{cc} 5^{40} \rightarrow & 3^{10} \\ & \downarrow \\ \cancel{20}6 & 2^{20} \\ & \downarrow \\ \cancel{30}1 & 8^{30} \end{array}\right)
\end{array}
$$

Total Transportation Cost =

$(40)(5) + (10)(3) + (20)(2) + (30)(8)$

$= 200 + 30 + 40 + 240$

$= 510$ prison guard hours.

The total cost of this initial basic feasible solution
is more than twice the optimal total cost!

An important problem facing many law enforcement
departments is that of providing adequate refueling
locations for various motorized units within a
specified command, so as to minimize lost patrol time,
assure the availability of fuel, and hopefully reduce
delays due to queueing for fuel. Consider the
following transportation problem, the numerical data
for which was adapted from a beer brewery problem

presented by Leon Cooper and David Steinberg.[1]

TABLE 5

A TRANSPORTATION PROBLEM FOR THE OPTIMAL
REFUELING OF MOTORIZED LAW ENFORCEMENT UNITS

Fuel Units Available	Fueling Location	20	60	80	40	10	Fuel Units Required
		I	II	III	IV	V	Motorized Units
50	A	7	3	2	4	2	
70	B	6	5	8	3	4	
90	C	3	2	5	7	1	

In a typical borough command in New York City
there may be only three locations (A, B, C), for
obtaining fuel, and there may be five motorized
units requiring fuel, I - emergency service units,
II - detective units, III - radio motorized patrol
(RMP) car and scooter units, IV - traffic and
motorcycle units, and V - supervisory units. Assume
that the values provided for supply and demand are
respectively, the average number of vehicles that
can be fueled up in a week, at an average load of
ten gallons per vehicle, and the average number of
vehicles per week that require fueling, also at

---

1 Leon Cooper and David Steinberg, Introduction to
Methods of Optimization (Philadelphia: W. B. Saunders
Co., 1970), 265.

an average load of ten gallons per vehicle.
The cost criterion in the measure matrix represents
the lost duty time as measured in quarter hours.
That is, the c_{11} entry of 7 indicates that each
vehicle from unit I sent to location A for refueling
loses, on the average, 7/4 hours of duty time.

Since this problem requires an allocation that
will minimize the total lost duty time of the units,
the transportation algorithm starts with step 2.
The tie in the c_{ij} minimum differences in the first
and third columns is resolved by taking second
differences which are respectively, 7-6 = 1 and
8-5 = 3. Thus, the first allocation is made to the
least cost in the third column because it has the
highest first and second differences.

	20	60	80	40	10	c_i
50	7	3	2^{50}	4	2	0
70	6	5	8	3	4	1
90	3	2	5	7	1	1
c_j	3	1	3	1	1	
	1		3			

An application of the other steps in the algorithm
yields the following initial basic feasible allocation. The T_i notation indicates the order in which
the allocations were assigned. The crossed out
supply and demand values represent adjustments

as allocations were made, and the crossed out
differences represent changes that were required
as rows and columns were completely allocated.

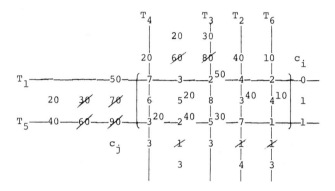

It should be noted that as the steps of the algorithm
were applied additional decisions (not necessarily
best or unique), were made when the minimum differences
were the same, and no second differences were available for comparison. For example , in deciding on the
third allocation between columns one and three, both
with minimum differences of three, column three was
selected for T_3 because its second choice of cost
$c_{23} = 8$ was higher than that of column one's, $c_{21}=6$.

This initial basic feasible allocation can now
be tested for optimality by using steps 6. through 8.
The results are summarized below.

$$
\begin{pmatrix}
7 & 3 & 2^{50} & 4 & 2 \\
6 & 5^{20} & 8 & 3^{40} & 4^{10} \\
3^{20} & 2^{40} & 5^{30} & 7 & 1
\end{pmatrix}
\begin{matrix} u_i \\ 0 \\ 6 \\ 3 \end{matrix}
\qquad
C^* =
\begin{pmatrix}
0 & -1 & 2 & -3 & -2 \\
\boxed{6} & 5 & \boxed{8} & 3 & 4 \\
3 & 2 & 5 & 0 & \boxed{1}
\end{pmatrix}
$$

v_j 0 -1 2 -3 -2

Since each $c_{ij}^* \leq c_{ij}$ the initial basic feasible
solution is also the optimal solution to the transportation problem. However, there are three c_{ij}^*
entries that are equal to c_{ij} entries even though
they carry zero allocations. Therefore, these three
entries, c_{21}, c_{23}, and c_{35} can be used as the basis
for deriving alternate optimal solutions with the same
total minimum cost. This point about alternate optimal
solutions is not mentioned in Cooper and Steinberg's[1]
discussion of the similar transportation problem.
In fact, when the point about alternate optimal
solutions is mentioned at all in the OR literature
on the transportation problem, no attempt is made
to enumerate them.

By using the incremental unit a, where
a = 0,1,2,3,...,n, all the optimal solutions with
the same total cost of 650 quarter-hours of lost
duty time can be enumerated. For example, the first

1 Cooper and Steinberg, 265-269.

set of alternate solutions indicates that for each allocation that is transferred from c_{22} to c_{21} there will be an increase of one quarter-hour of cost, but that this additional cost is balanced by each transfer of units from c_{31} to c_{32}, thereby resulting in a zero net change in total allocation costs. The results are summarized in Table 6.

There are a total of 62 alternate optimal solutions with a total duty time loss of 650 quarter-hours. These alternate optimal solutions represent about one-sixth the maximum total of 352 possible integer allocations for this problem as given by the inequality bound discussed earlier. Unlike some mathematical problem solutions that would be considered ambiguous if several different solutions were available, the alternate optimal solutions in this case should be welcomed by police executives, because they provide added flexibility to proposed plans for assigning motorized units to fueling locations.

TABLE 6

THE SIXTY-TWO ENUMERATED ALTERNATE OPTIMAL SOLUTIONS TO THE MOTORIZED LAW ENFORCEMENT REFUELING TRANSPORTATION PROBLEM

Number of
Independent
Optimal
Allocations

$$\begin{pmatrix} 7 & 3 & 2^{50} & 4 & 2 \\ 6^{a} & 5^{20-a} & 8 & 3^{40} & 4^{10} \\ 3^{20-a} & 2^{40+a} & 5^{30} & 7 & 1 \end{pmatrix} \quad a \leq 20 \qquad 21$$

$$\begin{pmatrix} 7 & 3 & 2^{50} & 4 & 2 \\ 6^{a} & 5^{20} & 8 & 3^{40} & 4^{10-a} \\ 3^{20-a} & 2^{40} & 5^{30} & 7 & 1^{a} \end{pmatrix} \quad a \leq 10 \qquad 10$$

$$\begin{pmatrix} 7 & 3 & 2^{50} & 4 & 2 \\ 6 & 5^{20-a} & 8^{a} & 3^{40} & 4^{10} \\ 3^{20} & 2^{40+a} & 5^{30-a} & 7 & 1 \end{pmatrix} \quad a \leq 20 \qquad 21$$

$$\begin{pmatrix} 7 & 3 & 2^{50} & 4 & 2 \\ 6 & 5^{20+a} & 8 & 3^{40} & 4^{10-a} \\ 3^{20} & 2^{40-a} & 5^{30} & 7 & 1^{a} \end{pmatrix} \quad a \leq 10 \qquad 10$$

Total number of independent optimal
allocations   62

Total minimal lost duty time in each allocation is 650 quarter-hours.

Conjectured total number of possible integer allocation is given by:

$$P \leq (3-1)(5-1) \text{ Max}(2,4) \text{ Min}(51,11)$$
$$P \leq (2)(4)(4)(11)$$
$$P \leq 352$$

CHAPTER VIII

THE PROBLEM OF SEQUENCING

The problem of sequencing involves the
arrangement of a set of tasks, tests, or procedures
into a specified order, so as to minimize criteria
such as completion time, overall cost, delays,
complaints, or to maximize criteria such as total
output, resource utilization, or efficiency. The
sequencing problem is an integral part of most of
the operations of the CJ system, and it has been the
concern of executives spanning a wide range of
interests from airline scheduling to the production
of zinc. While the more general problems of scheduling and coordination have received wide attention in
the literature and in practice, there are very few
explicit algorithms currently available which deal
with these problems, other than those which solve
some special cases of the sequencing problem.[1]

Historically, the first work in this area can
be traced to the so-called Gantt charts developed

1 Roger L. Sisson, "Sequencing Theory" in Progress in
Operations Research, Vol. I, ed. by R. L. Ackoff (New
York: John Wiley & Sons, Inc., 1966), 297.

around the turn of the century by the management
consultant, Henry L. Gantt (1861-1919). Gantt was
an associate of Frederick W. Taylor, and was known
primarily for his contributions to industrial
production control and project planning charts.
Gantt charts are basically qualitative in nature,
and they are used to identify the places in an operation where unnecessary delays and costs might occur.
By themselves, Gantt charts are unable to supply
quantitative methods for decreasing these delays
and costs. The first major breakthrough in providing
an algorithm for the optimal sequencing of n jobs
through a two step tandem operation (and with
certain restraints, a three stage tandem operation),
was established by S. M. Johnson in 1954.[1]

Since then, an extensive literature on sequencing
has been developed, along with a variety of applications, but remarkably little of it has produced new
algorithms for cases more general than those originally
considered by Johnson. The number of possible
sequence orderings increases quite rapidly with the
number of jobs (J) involved and the number of stages
or machines (M) in the production process. The number

---

1 S. M. Johnson, "Optimal Two and Three Stage Production Schedules with Setup Times Included," Naval
Research Logistics Quarterly, 1 (1954), 61-68.

of possible sequences is $(J!)^M$ when the M stages are
interchangeable, and J! when the ordering of M is fixed.
Consequently, most of the advances in sequencing
theory have involved the reduction in the number
of computational steps needed to obtain an optimal
sequence and/or the application of simulation
methods to obtain a feasible solution that is reasonably close to the true optimum.[1] One of the first
steps in this direction was provided by the important
observation of Harvey M. Wagner,[2] that many sequencing
problems could be represented by an integer linear
programming model.

It has been observed that the traveling salesman
problem also can be viewed as a sequencing problem.
As previously noted, the traveling salesman problem
also played a role in the development of the assignment
problem. This should indicate just how artificial
and limited it actually is to attempt to classify an
OR problem exclusively according to a particular
methodology. The role of computer simulation in

---

1 Russell L. Ackoff and Maurice W. Sasieni,
Fundamentals of Operations Research (New York:
John Wiley & Sons, Inc., 1968), 282.

2 H. M. Wagner, "An Integer Linear Programming Model
for Machine Scheduling," Naval Research Logistics
Quarterly, 6 (1959), 131-140.

the solution of sequencing problems was advanced by B. Giffler and G. L. Thompson[1]. The role of more subtle and dynamic considerations which are involved in the solution of large sequencing and traveling salesman problems was introduced by J. Heller.[2]

It should be noted that the term scheduling originally used by Johnson, is now generally referred to as sequencing since it involves the optimal ordering of a set of n jobs in a static way. By contrast, the term scheduling is used principally to imply not only the optimal ordering of a set of n jobs (sequencing), but that there are also added constraints to be met, such as certain calendar and queueing considerations for the n jobs. The still more general problem of coordination involves the scheduling of a variety of independently processed jobs which then have to be combined (coordinated), into a total overall optimal plan. Neither the problem of scheduling, nor that of coordination which involves the use of PERT (Program Evaluation Review Technique) and CPM (Critical Path Method),

---

1 B. Giffler and G. L. Thompson, "Algorithms for Solving Production-Scheduling Problems," Opns. Res., 8 (July-August, 1960), 487-503.

2 J. Heller, "Some Numerical Experiments for an M×J Flow Shop and its Decision-Theoretical Aspects," Opns. Res., 8 (March-April, 1960), 178-184.

are within the realm of this dissertation.[1]

Sequencing plays a part in almost every aspect of the CJ system. Some examples of sequencing problems occur in the ordered assignment of: police tours to duty rosters, judges to trial cases, forensic evidence to testing equipment, prosecutors to case preparations, and inmates to prison indoctrinations. In many CJ examples, the optimization considerations of the sequencing problem are overridden by the need to merely provide the "covering" criterion of assigning every job to be processed through a "machine" on a first in, first out basis (FIFO). This FIFO method of sequencing events, and the philosophy of merely providing coverage might have worked well in the past, but they have become increasingly ineffective and inefficient as the demands on the CJ system have increased.

The only study that dealt with the application of sequencing algorithms to the CJ system was done by Nelson B. Heller.[1] It involved developing models of optimal police manpower schedules by hour and day,

---

1 Consult, Ackoff and Sasieni, 275-303.

2 Nelson B. Heller, "Proportional Rotating Schedules," (unpublished Ph.D. dissertation, University of Pennsylvania, 1969).

through proportional considerations of geography and workload. However, the study was limited to the special case of n jobs (police personnel), processed through a one stage machine (the duty chart).

A typical problem in a forensic laboratory might involve a batch of evidence that has to be investigated (tested), and then to be documented (prepared), for court hearings. Assume that there are n jobs (types of evidence), that are to be processed through a two-stage operation (investigation and documentation). The problem is to minimize the total time needed for the overall preparation of the evidence through the two stages. The assumptions and limitations of this problem are compatible with those of the Johnson algorithm.

The assumptions required for the application of Johnson's two stage algorithm for sequencing problems can be summarized as follows, although some authors list considerably more assumptions, such as Sisson's eleven.[1]

1. The sequencing involves the processing of jobs (tasks tests, etc.), through two fixed and contingent stages in tandem with zero or constant transfer time between the stages.

---

1 Sisson, 298-299.

2. The processing time for each job at both stages
is known (in terms of average values or best
estimates), and the time remains constant regardless
of the job ordering.

3. The stages can handle only one job at a time without multiple processing, and once a job is begun it
cannot be transferred or delayed before its completion.

Consider the data expressed in hours, in Table 7
as a six job, two machine sequencing problem.

TABLE 7

THE INVESTIGATION AND DOCUMENTATION

OF FORENSIC EVIDENCE CONSIDERED AS A SIX JOB,

TWO STAGE SEQUENCING PROBLEM

Machine (Processing Stage)	Job (Type of Evidence)					
	(Blood) I	(Hair) II	(Fiber) III	(Finger-prints) IV	(Paint) V	(Tool Marks) VI
(Investigation) A	9	2	4	12	7	6
(Documentation) B	4	8	5	5	3	10

Since there are six jobs (J=6), and two machines (M=2),
there would be $(6!)^2$ or 518,400 alternatives to
consider if stages A and B were interchangeable.
Since they are not interchangeable in this example,

there are only 6! or 720 possible alternative
sequences to be considered -- a most arduous task
to complete by purely trial-and-error methods.
As an initial attempt to obtain an optimal solution,
assume that the evidence is processed in the order
given by Table 7.

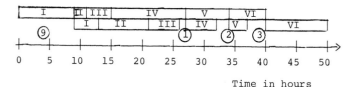

Time in hours

9 + 1 + 2 + 3 = 15 Hours of delay

Fig. 14 -- A Gantt chart for the initial solution
of the six job, two stage forensic science
sequencing problem.

An examination of the Gantt chart in Figure 14
indicates that the investigative unit has put in a
total of forty hours of work, and that this time
cannot be reduced since it represents the sum of the
process times for the six jobs taken consecutively
and immediately after the completion of each preceding
job. Under this sequencing order however, the documentation unit puts in fifty hours of work despite the
fact that the total sum of its process times is only
thirty-five hours. The excess fifteen hours developed

due to a nine hour delay before job I was ready
for documentation, and delays of one, two, and three
hours before documentation was possible on jobs IV,
V, and VI respectively. If a better sequencing order
is available, then it obviously must reduce these
delays or downtimes that occur during the processing
of stage B to a minimum.

A careful examination of Figure 14 leads to the
conclusion that the job with the smallest stage A
time should be processed first so as to minimize
the initial delay at stage B. The Johnson algorithm,
in modified form, for the two stage, n job sequencing
problem follows, where A represents the first stage
and B the second stage.

1. Select the lowest processing time of all the jobs,
in either stage.

2. If the processing time from step 1. appears in
stage A, then place its job at the beginning of the
sequence. If the least time appears in stage B, then
place its job at the end of the sequence. If two or
more times in the same stage are equal, then apply
the conditions of step 2. to the times in the other
stage.

3. Repeat steps 1. and 2., cross out jobs
already placed, and only consider those that remain
until all the jobs have been sequenced.

The optimal sequence will evolve toward the middle
from either end. In general, the sequence obtained
by this method is rarely unique, so that an exchange
of middle terms will usually yield alternate optimal
solutions.

Applying this elegantly simple algorithm to
the previous example produces the following optimal
sequence.

TABLE 8

AN OPTIMAL PROCESSING SEQUENCE FOR THE SIX
JOB, TWO STAGE FORENSIC EVIDENCE PROBLEM

Processing Order	1	2	3	4	5	6
Job	II	III	VI	IV	I	V
Stage A	2	4	6	12	9	7
Stage B	8	5	10	5	4	3

The jobs were assigned to their position in the
optimal sequence by the algorithm in the following
order: II, V, III, I, IV, VI. The Gantt chart
for this optimal sequence appears in Figure 15.

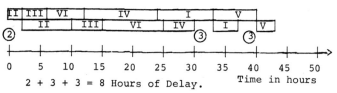

2 + 3 + 3 = 8 Hours of Delay.   Time in hours

Fig. 15 -- A Gantt chart for an optimal solution of
the six job, two stage forensic science sequencing problem.

The sequence illustrated in Figure 15 has resulted in a reduction of the total time in stage B from
fifty to forty-three hours, with the total saving
occurring in the reduction of the start up delay for
stage B from nine to two hours. The six hours of
down time during the actual processing of stage B
are unavoidably retained. It should be noted however,
that although the overall down time of eight hours is
minimal, the sequence that produced it is not unique.

For example, if the third (VI) and fourth (IV),
or the fourth (IV) and fifth (I) processed jobs are
reversed in the sequence, then the same eight hour
down time for stage B is obtained. These, and other
possible optimal sequences, provide equivalent alternatives to the one previously cited. Equivalent in
this case does not mean identical. For example,
the 3-4 reversal has four down periods compared to
only three for the 4-5 reversal. The 4-5 reversal
has a four hour down time which might be enough time
for a maintenance check, whereas the three hour
period of the 3-4 reversal might not suffice.

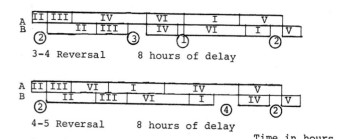

3-4 Reversal   8 hours of delay

4-5 Reversal   8 hours of delay

Fig. 16 -- Two alternate optimal solutions to the
forensic evidence sequencing problem
displayed by Gantt charts

The Johnson algorithm, while providing the
minimum total delay time at stage B, does not
provide the minimum interruption time during the
processing of stage B. In the previous example,
if job I were processed first, then stage B could
be run with no intermediate delays, and the total
down time would be concentrated at the beginning
of stage B's operations. The processing sequence
following this modification would be: I, II, III,
VI, IV, V, and its Gantt chart representation
appears in Figure 17.

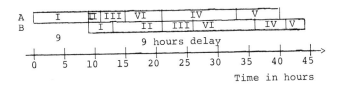

Fig. 17 -- A Gantt chart for an optimal solution to
the forensic evidence sequencing problem
that eliminates interruptions on stage B.

The total down time for stage B is increased by
one hour, to nine hours from eight hours. However,
the processing time for stage B is now accomplished
without interruption with the addition of only one
more hour of delay from start to finish (43 to 44
hours). This criterion of uninterrupted operation
for stage B may be as or more important than the
Johnson criterion of obtaining a total minimum delay
time for stage B.

However, there is no OR literature dealing with
the algorithm necessary for deriving an optimal
sequence based on eliminating interruptions during
the operations of stage B. The following additional
steps modify the Johnson algorithm so as to provide
an optimal sequence that satisfies the criterion of
having the minimum interruption time during the
operation of the second stage.

4. After establishing the Johnson sequence, draw the Gantt chart to determine the total delay units on stage $B(t_B)$.

5. Locate the time value in stage A that either equals t_B or is minimally larger than t_B, and place that job in the first position of the revised optimal sequence. In case there are two or more time entries in stage A that meet these conditions, select the one that has the largest stage B time value. If no value in stage A satisfies these conditions, then select the job with the largest stage A time value, and place it first in the revised optimal sequence.

The revised optimal sequence is now one with minimum time interruption during the processing on stage **B**. If the stage A time value of the job moved to the first position (A_i), in the revised optimal sequence is less than or equal to t_B, then the overall delay time at stage B is unchanged and the interruption during processing on stage B is given by $(t_B - A_i)$. However, if the stage A time value of the job moved to the first position of the revised optimal sequence is greater than t_B, then the overall delay is given by A_i, and the interruption time during the stage B processing is zero.

Johnson also proved that under certain conditions, his algorithm could be extended to three
tandem machines or stages processing n jobs. The
only additional assumption necessary for the extension
of the algorithm is that:
$\{Min\ (A_i) \geq Max\ (B_i)\}\ U\ \{Min\ (C_i) \geq Max\ (B_i)\}$,
where A, B, C is the order of job processing by
the machines. This mathematical formulation is
equivalent to the stated condition that the largest
value in the middle stage (B), must be less than or
equal to the smallest value in either the first stage
(A), or the last stage (C). If this last assumption
does not hold, then there is no algorithm currently
available that can be used to sequence the general
problem of n jobs to be processed on 3 tandem machines.
Nor is there a general algorithm of any sort when the
number of machines or stages is greater than three.

If the above mentioned assumption does hold,
then the n job, three machine sequencing problem can
be transformed into an n job two machine problem by
means of the following transformations:

$A^* = A_i + B_i$ $\qquad\qquad B^* = B_i + C_i$,

where A^* and B^* represent the transformed first and
second stages, respectively. The Johnson algorithm
now can be applied directly to the transformed problem
so as to obtain the optimal job sequence that will

yield the overall minimum processing time from start to finish through all the stages, or equivalently, that will yield a minimum down time in stage C.

Consider the following problem which involves the operation of a District Attorney's office. In processing various criminal cases for trial, it is found that basically three stages are involved. Stage A represents the gathering of evidence and testimony. Stage B represents the typing and cataloging of the data. Stage C represents the analysis and preparation of the cases for trial. Assume that the data for Table 9 was based on previous experience with similar cases and that the entries represent typical man-days of completion time. How should the cases be sequenced so as to minimize the total delay at stage C and therefore, on the entire operation?

TABLE 9

THE TYPICAL NUMBER OF MAN-DAYS FOR THE
DISTRICT ATTORNEY'S OFFICE TO PROCESS CRIMES
FOR COURT TRIAL EXPRESSED AS A FIVE JOB,
THREE MACHINE SEQUENCING PROBLEM

Processing Stage	Type of Crime				
	Murder I	Larceny II	Rape III	Misdemeanor IV	Burglary V
(Evidential) A	9	4	7	2	5
(Cataloging) B	3	2	2	1	1
(Preparation) C	4	4	5	3	6

To find the optimal sequence this three stage
sequence can be converted to a two stage sequence
since the largest value in B (B_1=3), is less than
or equal to the smallest value in either A or C
(C_4=3).

TABLE 10

CONVERSION OF THE FIVE JOB, THREE MACHINE
SEQUENCE PROBLEM TO A FIVE JOB, TWO MACHINE
SEQUENCING PROBLEM

	I	II	III	IV	V
A + B	12	6	9	3	6
B + C	7	6	7	4	7

An application of the Johnson algorithm to the data
of Table 10 produced the optimal sequence displayed
in Table 11.

TABLE 11

AN OPTIMAL PROCESSING SEQUENCE FOR THE FIVE
JOB, THREE STAGE DISTRICT ATTORNEY PROBLEM

Processing Order	1	2	3	4	5
Job Number	IV	V	II	III	I
A + B	3	6	6	9	12
B + C	4	7	6	7	7
A	2	5	4	7	9
B	1	1	2	2	3
C	3	6	4	5	4

The results of this optimal ordering are displayed
in Figure 18. It should be observed that the overall
processing time is thirty-four man-days, that the
total delay at stage B is twenty-one man-days, and
that the total delay at stage C is twelve man-days,
a minimum value.

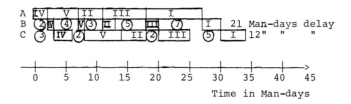

Fig. 18 -- A Gantt chart of the optimal sequence for
            the court trial preparation of five types
            of crime cases processed in three stages
            by the District Attorney's office.

The Johnson solution as illustrated in Figure 18,
has several drawbacks such as the fact that those
staff members who are assigned to stage B must endure
a total of nineteen of their twenty one down days
once their processing stage has begun, and similarly,
the personnel assigned to stage C must endure nine
of their twelve down days once their processing stage
has begun. An application of the modified Johnson
algorithm, as previously developed, will not yield a
reduction of the overall processing time of thirty-

four man-days or the minimum down time at stage C
of twelve hours. However, a switch of job I to the
first position in a revised optimal sequence as
illustrated in Figure 19, will reduce the overall
delay on stage B to twenty man-days with only eleven
man-days of   interim delay, and it will reduce
the interim delay at stage C to zero since $A_1 + B_1 = 12$,
the exact value of t_C.

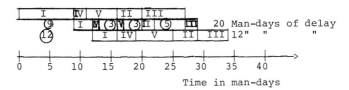

Fig. 19 -- A Gantt chart for the optimal sequencing
        of the District Attorney problem with
        minimal interim delay at stage C.

The optimal solution as given by the Johnson
algorithm is unaffected if each crime type were
reported as a member of the n jobs a finite number
of times. That is, if the n jobs consisted of
aI + bII + cIII + dIV + eV jobs, where the
coefficients are positive integers, then the original
Johnson solution would still be optimal by processing
d misdemeanors first, then e burglaries, then b
larcenies, then c rapes, and finally a murders.

It should be noted that the District Attorney may
not always be able to apply strictly rational
criteria to the sequencing of crime cases for trial.
Often the overriding criteria are produced by such
factors, as public opinion, pressure from the news
media, the preparedness of auxiliary agencies in the
CJ system, the necessities of priority considerations,
availability of staff, and the status of other cases.

As has been indicated previously, the problem
of sequencing n jobs over m machines, when $m \geq 3$,
is still unsolved by explicit algorithms. However,
such problems can be handled by computer simulation
methods which are designed to obtain feasible solutions
which are potentially or nearly optimal. There is
also a graphical method for handling the essentially
dual problem of sequencing two jobs through m
machines, so as to minimize the total completion time,
and where each job has a set order of machines through
which it must be processed.[1]

1 Consult, Ackoff and Sasieni, 281-282.

CHAPTER IX

THE PROBLEM OF QUEUEING

The phenomenon of queueing is familiar to
anyone who has waited on a movie line, brought a
car in for repairs, circled an airport, telephoned
into a switchboard, sat in a doctor's office,
checked out in a busy supermarket, paid a traffic
fine in person, or waited for a case to be judged.
The theory of queueing deals with the probabilistic
time delays associated with the rates of arrival
and service of customers using the facilities of
a system. A measure of effectiveness used in
queueing models involves finding an optimal balance
in cost between waiting customers and idle facilities.

A queue or line is said to exit whenever there
are customers waiting to use facilities, and in some
instances when there are idle facilities without
customers. In order to measure the cost of a queue,
weighted values, such as monetary cost, are assigned
to the time lost by waiting customers and idle
facilities. The problem of queueing is concerned
with providing the means to analyze such variables

as expected average delay, expected average number
in a queue, and the degree of facility utilization.
Unless one or more of the following items can be
controlled or modified, queueing theory can be used
only to describe the extent of a problem, and cannot
be used to reduce queue lengths and delays:

1. the customer arrival rate,

2. the facility service rate,

3. the number of service channels available for use,
    and

4. the discipline or priority in which arrivals are
    to be serviced.

   The typical queueing problem is stochastic in
nature, and unless it falls into very carefully
defined idealized models the analysis "...becomes
exceedingly complicated and very often even
intractable."[1] The queueing problems discussed
herein can be characterized by the following
assumptions which make up the well defined steady-
state queueing model of standard notation M/M/C.
These assumptions are reasonably well suited for
application to many operations in the CJ system.

---

1 Jagjit Singh, Great Ideas of Operations Research,
(New York: Dover Publications, Inc., 1968), 148.

1. The input is expressible in terms of Poisson
   arrival rates   (M/ /).

2. The output is expressible in terms of exponential
   service rates   (/M/).

3. The service is provided at a set of identical
   channels or stations   (/ /C).

4. The queueing discipline or service order is
   first-in, first-out (FIFO).

Other typical service orders are a random discipline
such as occurs in automatic telephone switching
networks, a priority discipline such as occurs in
the operation of a hospital emergency room, and
a last-in, first-out discipline (LIFO) such as occurs
in a preferential seniority rehiring system.

It is always possible to reduce customer queues
to practically zero, but that would require added service
channels which would then increase the idle time
periods and therefore, the cost of the service
facilities. Similarly, it is always possible to
reduce idle facilities to zero by cutting back on
the number of service channels, but that would
increase the queue length and therefore, increase
customer delays. Consequently, the solution of a
queueing problem usually consists of finding the
optimal balance between the expected costs of waiting
customers and the expected costs of idle facilities

with enough margin to account for unpredictable
fluctuations in the input and output characteristics
of the system.

One of the primary quantitative tools in the
St. Louis report[1] was the application of the queueing
theory model M/M/C, in order to predict police
manpower requirements for responding to service calls
based on an experimental study of resource allocations.
One aspect of that report provided a matrix table
over a given time period in which the predicted
number of calls for service were grouped into eight
major types that could be serviced by specified
assigned units.[2] Another tabulated result provided

> for each possible number of patrol units
> [grouped] ... by four-hour periods, the
> total number of predicted calls, the number
> and percentage which can be answered immedi-
> ately, the number and percentage which must
> wait to be serviced, and the increased number
> of calls which would be answered at once if
> one more unit were added.[3]

R. P. Shumate and R. F. Crowther[4] outlined

_____

1   Allocation of Patrol Manpower Resources
in the Saint Louis Police Department. 2 Vols.,
Thomas McEwen, Project Director, (St. Louis, Mo.:
St. Louis Police Department, July, 1966), Vol. II,
27-45.

2   Ibid., Vol. I, 9.

3   Ibid., Vol. I, 3.

4   R. P. Shumate and R. F. Crowther, "Quantitative
Methods for Optimizing the Allocation of Police
Resources," Journal of Criminal Law, Crimonology,
and Police Science, 57 (June, 1966), 197-206.

a method for applying queueing models to analyze
demands for police service. The study assumed a
Poisson distribution for the queueing model input,
which was the demand for police service. In order
to obtain the arrival rate(a), demand for police
service, the study divided the total number of
events in a given tour of duty over a one year
period by the total number of minutes in that tour
for the year. The study also developed a method
to approximate the probabilities of another event
occurring (for various values of a), before the one
in progress had been completed. A table based on
Erlangian formulas, was also developed to predict
estimated delay in minutes, and the probabilities
of various numbers of similar demands for police
service occurring simultaneously.

Frank C. Pethel and Donald Berilla,[2] also
used the M/M/C queueing model to describe the radio
communication system used by the Washington D. C.
Police Department. Formulas were developed for the
expected average number of calls in the system,and
the number of calls awaiting service as a function
of the utilization factor and the number of available
channels.

1   Frank C. Pethel and Donald Berilla, "A Communication
System for the Washington D. C. Police Department,"
in Law Enforcement Science and Technology I, ed. by
S. A. Yefsky (Washington, D. C.: Thompson Book Co.,
1967), 107-114.

Richard Larson[1] analyzed the operation of
the Boston Police Department's processing of calls
for police service. The police response system
consisted of a tandem of queueing models, each with
different priority disciplines. By assigning costs
to each priority, a weighted system mean response
time was developed which was then optimized with
the aid of a dynamic programming resource allocation
algorithm.

James Baker,[2] alluded to the effects of court
and correction queues in the CJ system. However,
the model he developed in this study is mainly one
based on linear inputs and constant feedback loops,
and as such does not squarely address the problem
of backlog queues that normally develop at various
points in the CJ system. The study by John B.
Jennings[3] did indicate the magnitude of such delays
in   New York City, and discussed their potential
improvement through the application of queueing methods.

1   Richard C. Larson, Operational Study of the Police
Response Time, Technical Report No. 26, (Cambridge,
Mass.: Operations Research Center, M. I. T., 1967).

2   James D. Baker, "On the Criminal Justice System,"
Law Enforcement Science and Technology II, ed. by
S. I. Cohn (Chicago: IIT Research Institute, 1969),
262-264.

3   John B. Jennings, The Flow of Defendants through the
New York City Criminal Court in 1967, RAND report
RM-6364-NYC, (New York: The RAND Institute,
September, 1970).

The following formulas are standard to the
M/M/1 (C=1, one service channel), queueing model
under the assumption that steady-state conditions
prevail.[1]

a = the expected number of arrived units per unit
   of time, and is the reciprocal of the average
   units of time between arrivals.

s = the expected number of served units per unit
   of time, and is the reciprocal of the average
   units of service time.

$u = \frac{a}{s}$ = the degree of system utilization, or the
   traffic intensity factor such that $0 \leq u < 1$.

$\bar{n} = \frac{u}{1-u}$, the expected (or average) number of units
   in the system as represented by those presently
   being served and those waiting in the queue.

$\bar{m} = u\bar{n} = \frac{u^2}{1-u}$, the expected (or average) number of
   units waiting in the queue.

$\bar{n} = \bar{m} + u$.

$\bar{w} = \frac{\bar{n}}{a} = \frac{1}{s(1-u)}$, the expected (or average) total··
   time spent in the system, from the time of a
   unit's arrival to the time of its departure.

$\bar{q} = u\bar{w} = \frac{\bar{n}}{s} = \frac{\bar{m}}{a} = \frac{u}{s(1-u)}$, the expected (or average)
   waiting time before service begins.

---

1 Consult, Samuel B. Richmond, Operations Research
for Management Decisions (New York: The Ronald Press
Co., 1968), 405-438, for the derivations of these
formulas.

$$\bar{w} = \bar{q} + \frac{1}{s}$$

$P_0 = (1-u)$, the probability that the queue length will be zero or that the facility will be idle.

$P_1 = u(1-u)$, the probability that there will be exactly one unit in the system.

$P_2 = u^2(1-u)$, the probability that there will be exactly two units in the system.

$\vdots$

$P_n = u^n(1-u)$, the probability that there will be exactly n units in the system.

$\sum_{i=0}^{n} P_i = P_0 + P_1 + P_2 + \ldots + P_n$, the probability that there will be n or less units in the system.

$1 - \sum_{i=0}^{n} P_i$, the probability that there will be more than n units in the system.

TABLE 12

A TABLE OF SELECTED VALUES BETWEEN THE

UTILIZATION FACTOR (U) AND THE EXPECTED

TOTAL NUMBER OF UNITS ($\bar{N}$) IN AN M/M/1

QUEUEING SYSTEM

u	.1	.2	.3	.4	.5	.6	.7	.8	.9	.95	.99	1.0
$\bar{n}$	.11	.25	.43	.67	1.0	1.5	2.3	4.0	9.0	18	99	∞

For $c > 1$, then $u' = u/c$, and the preceding formulas are modified by u' accordingly.

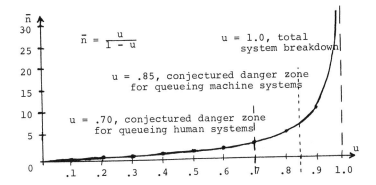

Fig. 20 -- A graph of u versus $\bar{n}$ in an M/M/1 queue
          with certain critical utilization values
          indicated.

Any M/M/1 queueing system that operates such that
$u \geq .8$ is critically close to complete breakdown even
though there appears to be a twenty percent capacity
remaining. This should be evident from an examination
of the data in Table 12, and the graph in Figure 20. The
principal reason for the rapid increase in $\bar{n}$ as u
approaches one, is due to the stochastic nature of
the arrival and service times, which in practice do
not exhibit the orderliness of the average values
used to obtain the utilization factor u. The OR
literature does not differentiate between critical
utilization factors for queueing systems that are
primarily humanistic, and those that are primarily

mechanistic. It is conjectured, in Figure 20, that
the critical u level for human queueing systems is
reached far earlier than the critical u level for
machine queueing systems.

The following example is an application of the
queueing theory M/M/1 model to one junction point
in the processing flow of persons moving through the
CJ system. The data in Table 13 represents the
number of felony cases that are arraigned with a not
guilty plea, and the number of cases tried with
court verdicts handed down, for a representative set
of working days in a given month for a certain jurisdiction. The court system in this example, is set up
so that once the felony case has been arraigned with
a plea of not guilty, the felony case can be considered as an "arrival", and immediately sent to a
single court channel in order to receive a trial
with verdict, which when completed can be considered
as a "service".

TABLE 13

NUMBER OF FELONY ARRAIGNMENTS WITH NOT GUILTY

PLEA AND NUMBER OF FELONY TRIALS WITH VERDICT

IN A MONTH FOR A REPRESENTATIVE JURISDICTION

Working Day of the Month	1	2	3	4	5	6	7	8	9	10	11	12	13	14	15	16	17	18	19	20	21	22	23
Number of Arraignments with a not guilty plea (a_i)	6	4	3	0	1	1	2	0	2	3	4	3	2	0	2	1	7	2	1	5	1	3	2
Number of trials with verdicts handed down (s_i)	2	3	2	4	2	6	5	7	3	3	2	2	4	6	5	2	7	3	4	2	5	8	3

Since the criminal court system is basically
a dynamic one, as are most of the other parts of the
CJ system, no attempt is made at establishing a one-
to-one correspondence between incoming cases and
outgoing cases in this queueing model. In fact, to
do so in a real situation is virtually impossible,
and the only realistic approach is to consider net
flow figures through the court channel. Ultimately
of course, served cases must balance arrivals and

the conditions of Figure 21, cannot continue to prevail. It is also assumed for convenience, that the court system has just one service channel even though there may be more than one judge presiding per day. This is accomplished by considering the total court output figures as an output from a single channel (C = 1, in the M/M/C queueing model).

Input   Output

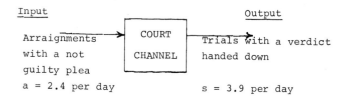

Arraignments → COURT   Trials with a verdict
with a not   CHANNEL   handed down
guilty plea
a = 2.4 per day   s = 3.9 per day

Fig. 21 -- A black box model representation of
         a court queueing system.

Using the previously described formulas for an M/M/1 queueing model, the following court system values are obtained from the data in Table 13.

$a = \dfrac{\sum a_i}{n} = 55/23 = 2.39 \approx 2.4$ (average number of arraignments per day with a not guilty plea)

$s = \dfrac{\sum s_i}{n} = 90/23 = 3.91 \approx 3.9$ (average number of verdicts handed down per day)

$u = \dfrac{a}{s} = 2.4/3.9 = .615 \stackrel{\sim}{\sim} .62$ (court system's

utilization factor)

$\bar{n} = \dfrac{u}{1-u} = .62/(1-.62) = 1.63 \stackrel{\sim}{\sim} 1.6$ (average number

of felony defendants in the court system)

$\bar{m} = u\bar{n} = .62(1.6) = .992 \stackrel{\sim}{\sim} 1.0$ (average number of

felony defendants awaiting trail)

$\bar{w} = \bar{n}/a = 1.6/2.4 = .67 \stackrel{\sim}{\sim} .7$ (average number of

days felony defendant spends in the court

system)

$\bar{q} = \bar{n}/s = 1.6/3.9 = .41 \stackrel{\sim}{\sim} .4$ (average number of days

felony defendant has to wait before trial)

TABLE 14

TABLE OF PROBABILITIES THAT A FELONY

DEFENDANT QUEUE WILL BE EXACTLY OF LENGTH n

n	0	1	2	3	4	5	6	7
P_n	.38	.24	.15	.09	.06	.03	.02	.01

$\displaystyle\sum_{i=0}^{7} P_i = \sum_{n=0}^{7} u^n(1-u) = .98$ (cumulative probability

that the felony defendant queue will be of

length seven or less)

-204

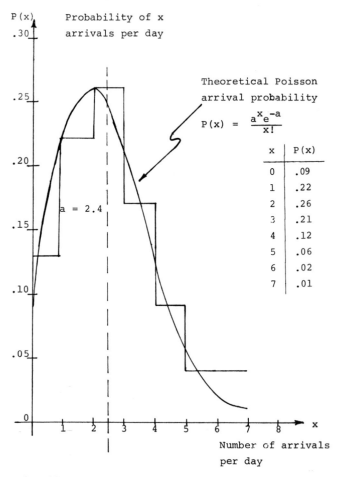

Fig. 22 -- Probability of felony defendant arrivals
per day into a criminal court system.

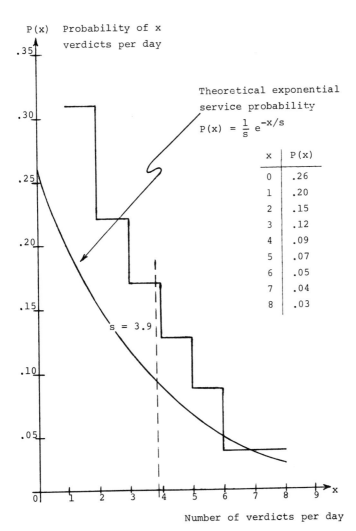

P(x) Probability of x
verdicts per day

Theoretical exponential
service probability

$$P(x) = \frac{1}{s} e^{-x/s}$$

x	P(x)
0	.26
1	.20
2	.15
3	.12
4	.09
5	.07
6	.05
7	.04
8	.03

s = 3.9

Number of verdicts per day

Fig. 23 -- Probability of felony defendant verdicts
per day in a criminal court system.

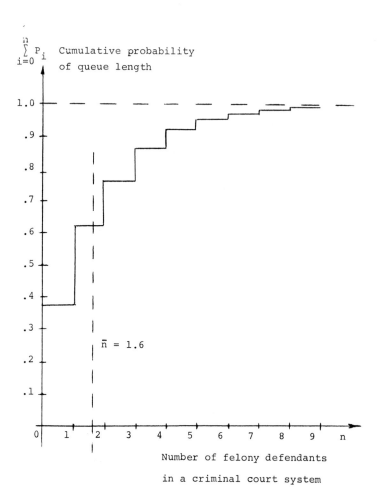

Fig. 24 -- Cumulative probability that there will be
n felony defendants or less in a criminal
court system queue.

From the preceding calculations it is reasonable
to assume that the court system in the example is
well under control since the cumulative probability
that there are no more than four felony defendants
in the queue is .92. However, this analysis assumes
that the input and output data are in steady-state
conditions, and that the utilization factor is
relatively stable. If arrivals should increase, or
service should decrease, or both occur simultaneously,
then the queue stability could be radically altered.
Table 15 summarizes various possible outcomes for
the court system parameters s, $\bar{n}$, $\bar{q}$, and P_n as functions of increasing u values, when a is held constant
at 2.4.

TABLE 15

A SUMMARY OF VARIOUS OUTCOMES FOR THE COURT
SYSTEM QUEUE AS A FUNCTION OF THE UTILIZATION
FACTOR WITH ARRIVALS HELD CONSTANT

u	s	$\bar{n}$	$\bar{q}$	P_0	P_1	P_2	P_3	P_4	P_5	P_6	P_7	$\sum_{i=0}^{7} P_i$
.62	3.9	1.6	.4	.38	.24	.15	.09	.06	.03	.02	.01	.98
.70	3.4	2.3	.7	.30	.21	.15	.10	.07	.05	.04	.02	.94
.75	3.2	3.0	.9	.25	.19	.14	.10	.08	.06	.04	.03	.89
.80	3.0	4.0	1.3	.20	.16	.13	.10	.08	.07	.05	.04	.83
.85	2.8	5.7	2.0	.15	.13	.11	.09	.08	.07	.06	.05	.74
.90	2.7	9.0	3.3	.10	.09	.08	.07	.07	.06	.05	.05	.57
.95	2.5	19.0	7.6	.05	.05	.04	.04	.04	.04	.03	.03	.32
.99	2.4^+	99.0	41.0	.01	.01	.01	.01	.01	.01	.01	.01	.08

All table values based on a = 2.4.

It is not uncommon for criminal court systems
to have waiting times above seven days before trial.
In fact, Joseph A. Navarro and Jean G. Taylor,[1]
reported that the 1965 data for the District of
Columbia criminal court system had a mean waiting
period of 19 weeks (133 days), with a median of
15 weeks, and a maximum of 61 weeks! Similarly long
delays occur in practically all large metropolitan
criminal court systems. It is obvious that such
jurisdictions are operating well above a .99 utilization factor, and consequently they are very near
to a condition of complete queue instability, if
not total collapse.

The only way to reduce such potentially dangerous
queue lengths (assuming of course that there is no
reduction in the arrival of arraignments), would
be to add more service channels in the form of judges,
courtrooms, and all the associated auxiliary staff
and equipment necessary. However, such patchwork
attempts to reduce backlogs in one aspect of the CJ
system could lead to a suboptimization fallacy, since
"... in a dynamic system removal of one bottleneck
often shows up another elsewhere."[2] In this case,

---

1 Joseph A. Navarro and Jean C. Taylor, "Data
Analyses and Simulation of Court System in the
District of Columbia for the Processing of Felony
Defendants," in Task Force: SAT, 206.
2 Singh, 133.

increased efficiency at the courtroom trial level
alone would only tend to further aggrevate the
already heavy queue conditions at the sentencing,
incarceration, probation, and parole levels.

CHAPTER X

THE METHOD OF SIMULATION

The method of simulation involves the
imitation of a concept, device, process, or system.
Simulation is usually carried out as an analogy to
the reality it seeks to model. The simulation model
is often more probabilistic in structure than
deterministic, due to the amorphous nature of the
subject being modeled. Imitation is often
considered the highest form of flattery, but to
the OR analyst, simulation may have to be the
highest form of appeal when all other modeling
methods have proven inadequate.

Table 16 is an expansion and a modification
of the suggestion by Dimitris N. Chorafas,[1] that
the various methods of solving system problems can
be classified according to four categories, and
grouped into a 2 × 2 matrix. The methods of solving
system problems are rarely so clear cut, and obviously

---

1 Dimitris N. Chorafas, Systems and Simulation,
(New York: Academic Press, 1965), 17-23.

there are many overlapping techniques among the
four categories. The point to be emphasized however, is that the classification of a system problem
into the category that requires the method of
simulation for solution usually occurs when both
the data from the real system and the model imitation
of the real system are principally probabilistic in
nature.

TABLE 16

A CLASSIFICATION OF SYSTEM PROBLEM SOLUTION
METHODS INTO FOUR CATEGORIES BASED ON THE
DETERMINISTIC-PROBABLISTIC FORM OF THE DATA
AND MODELS

Data from the Real System	Model Imitation of the Real System	
	Deterministic	Probabilistic
Deterministic	Analysis	Iteration
Probabilistic	Statistics	Simulation

Simulation is necessary and advisable in the
analysis of systems, when one or more of the following
conditions apply:

1. the system is only partially understood or
exceedingly complex,

2. the system is new, proposed, or non-existent,

3. the analytical formulation of the problem is
unwieldy or unattainable,

4. there are a large number of poorly defined variables,

5. there is a great deal of undifferentiable interdependence among the variables,

6. the objectives are to predict outcomes, to verify projections, to perform experimentation, or to train personnel without interfering with the system's operations,

7. to develop an operational model of the system,

8. to experiment on the actual system would be too costly,

9. to manipulate the actual system would be too lengthy, impractical, or counterproductive, and

10. the system is so unstable or variable that feasible solutions require constant monitoring and reevaluation.

The mathematical models of simulation, especially those involving the aid of electronic computers, are of recent origin, despite the fact that the concept of studying problems by analog simulation is a relatively old one. The concept of simulation is involved in many activities such as food tasting, stress testing, wear testing, scale models, flight simulators, athletic conditioning, and educational and professional training.

Mathematical simulation can be classified
into two broad areas -- the analog and the digital.
These two classifications approximate the classical
partitioning of numbers by the Pythagoreans into
the continued (used to study geometry and astronomy),
and the discrete (used to study arithmetic and music).
Analog simulation involves the use of a continuous
yardstick, such as the flow of current in an electrical network, in order to simulate the behavior of a
different phenomenon, such as a vibrating mechanical
spring. Digital simulation involves the use of a
finite generating device, such as Comte de Buffon's
method of dropping pins of length d onto a flat
plane marked off with parallel lines 2d units apart,
in order to approximate the value of π as the ratio
of total pins dropped to total lines touched. Modern
simulation methods incorporate the best aspects of
the analog and digital methods of simulation into a
hybrid form of simulation which makes use of modern
high speed electronic computers.

The origins of digital simulation methods can be
traced to the work of John von Neumann[1] who, along

---

1   Robert D. Richtmyer   and John von Neumann,
"Statistical Methods in Neutron Diffusion," in
John von Neumann: Collected Works, Vol. V, ed. by
A. H. Taub (New York: The Macmillan Co., 1963), 751-764.

with Stanislaw Ulam, is credited with developing
a technique code named "Monte Carlo," during World
War II, which was used to analyze atomic chain
reactions in nuclear piles. The Monte Carlo method[1]
has its roots in the "drunkard's random walk" problem.
This classic mathematical problem begins with a drunk
holding onto a lamppost, and involves determining the
probability that he will be able to get to within a
block of his home. The drunk is allowed to walk only
along streets and avenues, and thus his movements
can be conveniently represented by the grid lines of
the conventional Cartesian coordinate system. The
drunkard's walk (which is actually a random stagger),
is supposed to simulate (or vice versa), the probability
that a neutron of known initial direction and energy
will penetrate to a specified depth into a medium
of known atomic composition and geometric structure.[2]

Most problems that require the use of simulation
are beyond hand calculations, and therefore, must be

1 Consult, Herbert A. Meyer, ed., Symposium on Monte
Carlo Methods (New York: John Wiley & Sons, Inc.,
1956).

2 Consult, George W. Morgenthalier, "The Theory and
Application of Simulation in Operations Research,"
in Progress in Operations Research, Vol. I, ed. by
R. L. Ackoff (New York: John Wiley & Sons, Inc., 1966),
387-393.

programmed into computer languages in order to use
the speed and capacity of electronic computers for
their solution. These program languages vary from
the complex but flexible SIMSCRIPT[1] which uses For-
tran, to the simple but restricted GPSS (General
Purpose Systems Simulator).[2]

One of the first applications of simulation to
the CJ system described the use of computer simulation for law enforcement problems in general, and for
assisting in the evaluation of an automatic license
plate scanning system in particular.[3] Navarro and
Taylor[4] described a simulation model based on
observed data, for the processing of felony defendants
in the District of Columbia trial court system.
The COURTSIM simulation model they discussed was
designed to measure the impact on reducing court delays,

1 Harry M. Markowitz, Bernard Hausner, and Herbert
W. Karr, SIMSCRIPT: A Simulation Programming Language,
(Englewood Cliffs, N. J.: Prentice-Hall, 1965).

2 International Business Machine Corp., General
Purpose Systems Simulator II, Reference Manual
B20-6346-1 (Poughkeepsie, N. Y.: IBM Data Processing
Division, 1963),

3 William A. Wallace, "Computer Simulation and Law
Enforcement: An Application to the Automobile Theft
Problem," in Law Enforcement Science and Technology I,
ed. by S. A. Yefsky (Washington, D.C.: Thompson Book
Co., 1967), 629-634.

4 Navarro and Taylor, in Task Force: SAT, 199-215.

and on the availability of resources within the
court system, through a manipulation of potential
organizational and procedural changes.

In a report adapted from the author's Ph.D.
dissertation, Larson,[1] provided a general simulation
model in order to examine current and alternative
police dispatch-patrol systems. The work was done
within a hypothetical city and command structure,
although it was based on first hand experience in
the Boston and New York City police jurisdiction.
A simulation model was used to develop reasonably
optimal methods for the allocation of police resources
to various patrol deployment strategies under routine
conditions, and to various dispatch and reassignment
policies under emergency conditions.

A report designed to demonstrate the suitability
and usefulness of computer simulation in the analysis
and design of New York City's police response system
was developed by Norbert Hauser, et al.[2] The report,
though based on the New York City emergency response
system before the institution of the 911 emergency

---

1 Richard C. Larson, Models for the Allocation of
Urban Police Patrol Forces, Technical Report No. 44
(Cambridge, Mass.: Operations Research Center,
M. I. T., 1969).

2 Norbert Hauser, Gilbert R. Gordon, and Julius Surkis,
"Computer Simulation of a Police Emergency Response
System, Project No. 030, a report prepared for the
U. S. Dept. of Justice, Law Enforcement Administration,
(New York: Polytechnic Institute of Brooklyn, Sept.,
1969).

number and the computerized SPRINT system, was
nevertheless, general enough to be of value in
understanding the present New York Police experience
in this area, and was flexible enough for potential
application to other jurisdictions. By specifying
various incoming call rates, simulation models were
used to predict the required number of switchboard
operators, the average waiting time per call, and
the fraction of the time that the telephone circuits
were busy.

Nelson B. Heller and Richard Kolde,[1] presented
a paper which used GPSS language to simulate the
operation of the St. Louis Metropolitan Police
Department's real-time motor vehicle inquiry system.
By simulating the alternation of terminal equipment,
the message assembly procedure, the priority system,
and the system loading, they were able to demonstrate
the potential for an increased system capacity, and
a reduced system response time.

The Monte Carlo method will be outlined through
an example, in order to illustrate the potential use
of simulation techniques in the analysis of CJ system

---

1 Nelson B. Heller and Richard Kolde, "The Use of
Simulation in Planning Expansion of the St. Louis
Police Real-Time Motor Vehicle Inquiry System,"
(paper presented at the 38th national meeting of
the ORSA, Detroit, Mich., October 30, 1970).

problems. Table 17 depicts the known, average
probability distributions for the number of service
calls as a function of time measured in minutes,
for each of three police precincts. It is assumed
that the statistical variance of the data is relatively small over the time period under study. The
problem is to predict or estimate the effects on
service call distributions, as a result of combining
the three existing police precincts into various
new precinct formations which have no previous service
call history of their own.

TABLE 17

PROBABILITY DISTRIBUTIONS OF INCOMING CALLS
FOR SERVICE TO THREE EXISTING POLICE PRECINCTS

Minutes between calls for service	Police Precinct		
	A	B	C
1	.00	.01	.00
2	.00	.05	.00
3	.02	.25	.00
4	.10	.30	.05
5	.40	.20	.20
6	.30	.15	.20
7	.05	.04	.25
8	.00	.00	.25
9	.10	.00	.05
10	.03	.00	.00

The key to the application of the Monte Carlo method depends upon assigning random digits in proportion to the probability distributions of the calls for service in each of the three police precincts. Since the statistics in Table 17 are given in hundredths, the set of random digit assignments from 00 to 99 inclusive, will suffice in this case.[1] The random digits have been assigned in Table 18, in a cumulative fashion but always in exact proportion to the corresponding probability statistics of Table 17. The net effect of Table 18 is to transfer the statistics of Table 17 out of the real world, and into a purely numerical sample space designed to simulate incoming calls for police service at the three precincts based on the call pattern histories.

---

1 Consult, RAND Corp., A Million Random Digits with 100,000 Normal Deviates (hereinafter Random Digits), (New York: The Free Press, 1955), xi-xxv, for details on the generation and application of random digits.

TABLE 18

RANDOM DIGIT ASSIGNMENTS FOR THE PROBABILITY

DISTRIBUTIONS OF INCOMING CALLS FOR SERVICE

TO THREE EXISTING POLICE PRECINCTS

Minutes between Calls for Service	Police Precinct		
	A	B	C
1	–	00	–
2	–	01-05	–
3	00-01	06-30	–
4	02-11	31-60	00-04
5	12-51	61-80	05-24
6	52-81	81-95	25-44
7	82-86	96-99	45-69
8	–	–	70-94
9	87-96	–	95-99
10	97-99	–	–

With the aid of a random digit generator, the entire service call operation can be simulated at the three existing police precincts, or any combination of the three, into proposed new precincts, without affecting actual operations or costing anything in terms of personnel, equipment, safety, risk, or money. The limitations on the adequacy of the final simulated results will depend upon the accuracy of the generating statistics, the selection method for the random digits, the length of the simulation run, and the stability of the system's demand for service.

Table 19 represents the simulated run of twenty-five separate calls for police service at each of the three precincts, and the various combined outcomes for the proposed new precincts (AB, AC, BC, and ABC). Each random digit selection (R_a, R_b, R_c), was then translated to its minute interval equivalent (M_a, M_b, M_c), by reference to Table 18. The combined minute interval entries were obtained by selecting the minimum value from the appropriate M_a, M_b and M_c data of each line. The random digits were obtained from Random Digits.[1]

---

1 Random Digits, 362, lines 18050-18074, and columns 1, 5, 9.

TABLE 19

A MONTE CARLO SIMULATION RUN TO PREDICT THE
DISTRIBUTION OF CALLS FOR SERVICE CHARACTER-
ISTICS AT FOUR PROPOSED POLICE PRECINCTS TO
BE DERIVED FROM VARIOUS COMBINATIONS OF THREE
EXISTING PRECINCTS

Sample Number	Existing Police Precincts						Proposed Police Precincts			
	A		B		C		AB	AC	BC	ABC
	R_a	M_a	R_b	M_b	R_c	M_c	Min (M_a, M_b)	Min (M_a, M_c)	Min (M_b, M_c)	Min (M_a, M_b, M_c)
1	64	6	96	7	09	5	6	5	5	5
2	07	4	84	6	36	6	4	4	6	4
3	13	5	11	3	14	5	3	5	3	3
4	14	5	87	6	01	4	5	4	4	4
5	09	4	98	7	27	6	4	4	6	4
6	46	5	05	2	83	8	2	5	2	2
7	52	6	42	4	32	6	4	6	4	4
8	21	5	96	7	04	4	5	4	4	4
9	63	6	37	4	39	6	4	6	4	4
10	73	6	75	5	99	9	5	6	5	5
11	57	6	80	5	37	6	5	6	5	5
12	83	7	24	3	78	8	3	7	3	3
13	77	6	45	4	94	8	4	6	4	4
14	01	3	17	3	83	8	3	3	3	3
15	78	6	87	6	60	7	6	6	6	6
16	72	6	16	3	47	7	3	6	3	3
17	25	5	62	5	66	7	5	5	5	5
18	69	6	09	3	86	8	3	6	3	3
19	84	7	20	3	31	6	3	6	3	3
20	53	6	88	6	37	6	6	6	6	6
21	54	6	55	4	83	8	4	6	4	4
22	51	5	14	3	64	7	3	5	3	3
23	35	5	05	2	21	5	2	5	2	2
24	00	3	86	6	36	6	3	3	6	3
25	79	6	95	6	90	8	6	6	6	6

The simulation results of Table 19 are tabulated by frequency and probability distributions in Table 20, and they are graphed in Figures 25-27. It should be noted that a Monte Carlo run of twenty-five simulated calls for service at each existing police precinct is hardly sufficient to obtain a reliable prediction of the service call distributions at the proposed police precincts, and that a larger computerized run would be preferable in an actual system simulation. Nevertheless, even with this small sample run, it should be evident that Monte Carlo simulation is a powerful predictive and analytical tool, of relatively low cost and high output, which does not interrupt a system's normal operations during its testing process. The data contained in Table 20 could have been obtained by strictly analytical methods involving probabilities and combinations. However, the use of Monte Carlo methods provides the advantages of:

1. stopping the run at any time, and observing the progress of the simulation as it proceeds,

2. simplified calculations, and the ease of transfer to computerized methods, and

3. flexibility of introducing new input data, and requesting additional output data.

TABLE 20

FREQUENCY AND PROBABILITY DATA FOR THE MONTE

CARLO SIMULATION OF THE NUMBER OF MINUTES

BETWEEN CALLS FOR POLICE SERVICE AT FOUR

PROPOSED PRECINCTS

Simu-lated Minutes be-tween service Calls	Proposed Police Precincts							
	AB		AC		BC		ABC	
	Freq.	Prob.	Freq.	Prob.	Freq.	Prob.	Freq.	Prob.
1	0	–	0	–	0	–	0	–
2	2	.08	0	–	2	.08	2	.08
3	8	.32	2	.08	7	.28	8	.32
4	6	.24	4	.16	6	.24	8	.32
5	5	.20	6	.24	4	.16	4	.16
6	4	.16	12	.48	6	.24	3	.12
7	0	–	1	.04	0	–	0	–
8	0	–	0	–	0	–	0	–

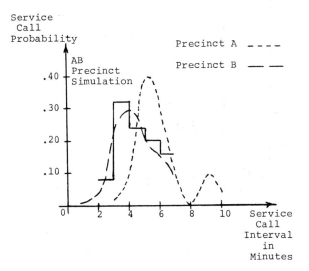

Fig. 25 -- Graph of the Monte Carlo simulation of
probabilities for police service calls
at minute intervals for the proposed
AB precinct.

-226-

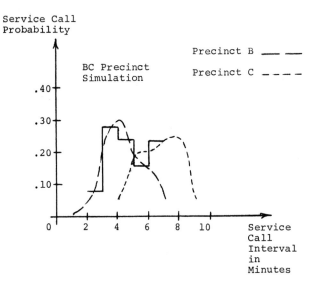

Fig. 26 -- Graph of the Monte Carlo simulation
of probabilities for police service calls
at minute intervals for the proposed BC
precinct.

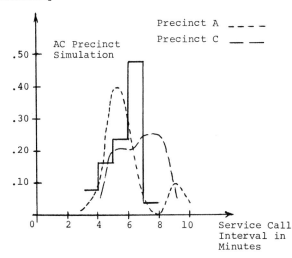

Fig. 27 -- Graph of the Monte Carlo simulation
of probabilities for police service
calls at minute intervals for the
proposed AC precinct.

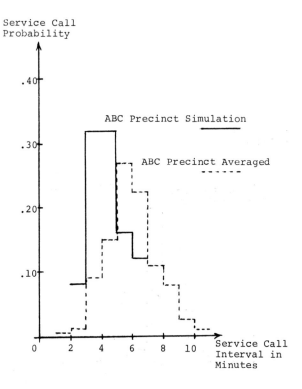

Fig. 28 -- Graph of the Monte Carlo Simulation
of probabilities for police service calls
at minute intervals for the proposed ABC
precinct versus the averaged ABC precinct
probabilities.

It is important to note that due to the
stochastic nature of problems involving calls for
police service, as well as most other CJ system
problems suitable for simulation analysis, it would
have been inaccurate and inconclusive merely to
have averaged the original probability distributions
appearing in Table 17 for the existing police
precincts, as indicated in Table 21, in order to
simulate the service call behavior of the proposed
new precincts. The simulated ABC precinct versus
the averaged ABC precinct are graphed in Figure 28.
The characteristics of the averaged ABC precinct
are wholly artificial, unreliable, and bear only
coincidental similarity to the simulated ABC
distribution.

TABLE 21

AVERAGED PROBABILITY DATA FOR THE MINUTES

BETWEEN SERVICE CALLS AT THE PROPOSED

POLICE PRECINCTS

Minutes between Service Calls	Proposed Police Precincts			
	AB	AC	BC	ABC
1	.005	.000	.005	.003
2	.025	.000	.025	.017
3	.135	.010	.125	.090
4	.200	.075	.175	.150
5	.300	.200	.200	.267
6	.225	.250	.175	.217
7	.045	.150	.145	.113
8	.000	.125	.125	.083
9	.050	.075	.025	.050
10	.015	.015	.000	.010

SUMMARY AND CONCLUSIONS

There is still no universally accepted definition of operations research. OR methods and
techniques span a wide range of disciplines from
the physical to the social sciences. Consequently,
OR definitions often are tailored to satisfy a
particular subject application. Since OR emerged
as a distinct discipline within the past thirty years,
it is still in its formative stages. Thus, the
acceptance of a definitive definition is unlikely
at present, and undesirable for the future extension
of OR to new areas. Nevertheless, the following
definition of OR represents a broad blend of the
many definitions appearing in the literature.

> OR is an interdisciplinary, scientific
> approach to the solution of problems that
> involve the complex, dynamic, and subjective
> interaction of men, methods, and systems which
> are generally unyielding to exact solution by
> purely analytic or trial-and-error techniques.
> By using mathematical modeling as a primary
> resource, OR methodology is designed to quantify
> and bound these problems within the framework
> of certain implied or specified constraints,
> measures, objectives, and variables, so as
> to seek optimal operating controls, decisions,
> levels, and solutions.

The essential ingredients necessary in an OR
study may be summarized by the 10M criterion: the
manipulation of mathematical models in order to
measure the management of men, machines, methods
and money in their milieu. Although there is some
controversy over the issue, it seems clear that
A. P. Rowe should be given credit as the first one
to label such studies as operational research.
There is no controversy over the credit to be given
to the American conversion of the phrase operational
research to that of operations research. This
distinction belongs to Philip M. Morse.

As with most any other pursuit, OR did not
emerge spontaneously as a fully developed discipline.
In Chapter I, its roots were traced to early Biblical
references, and its origins were identified in
various great feats of ancient history. Archimedes
can be regarded as the first true practitioner of OR
in a modern sense, while Plato can be regarded as
the first OR philosopher.

Until the twentieth century, the development of
OR had been in the shadows of the development of the
scientific method. It was not until there was a clear
need to include in the analyses of problems such
intangible and difficult to measure factors as those
involved in human and social activities, that OR

was able to take an independent stance of its own.
The actual impetus for the creation of OR was supplied
by problems that forced a socialization of the
scientific method in order to provide a means of
handling many more variables than were typical of
physical science problems. The methodology of OR
encompasses everything in the standard scientific
method, as well as other currently available
techniques including heuristics, simulation, game
theory, and interdisciplinary analysis. It seems
clear that OR has perfected, and superceded the
scientific method as a means of studying dynamic
system problems. OR is certainly the only method
currently available that allows for the study of
problems within their environmental surroundings
without isolating a part of the system as is the
usual practice in the scientific method of laboratory
or experimental studies.

There have been many investigators who can be
listed among the early formulators of modern OR theory.
From the many eligible for such distinction, seven
were selected for discussion in Chapter II, as the
most deserving, as well as the fact that their
contributions were representative of the interdisciplinary development and nature of OR. Charles
Babbage developed the forerunner of the modern computer

as a practical means of bypassing human errors in the production of mathematical tables. Frederick W. Taylor was one of the earliest business consultants who demonstrated the value of experimentation and data analysis as a means of improving corporate efficiency. A. K. Erlang created the first mathematical OR model by developing the theory of queueing to explain certain aspects of telephone networks. Thomas A. Edison popularized the research laboratory approach to system problems, and did some of the first nationally commissioned studies on improving military tactics. Frederick W. Lanchester applied the talents which he had used to perfect the automobile and anticipate the modern airplane, to devise a mathematical model to predict the outcome between competing forces. Horace C. Levinson was the first one to demonstrate the value of applying systematic analyses to retail sales operations. Erich Schneider, though not the first one to apply scientific methods to economics, was the first one to demonstrate the role of linear and quadratic programming in the solution of OR cost models.

The slow, imperceptible, and often groping emergence of OR over a period of many centuries was greatly accelerated by the advent of World War II.

Necessity, in this case, was both mother and father
in the creation of OR in Great Britain during the
late 1930s. OR originally developed to overcome
the problems surrounding the installation and use
of RADAR, soon spread to practically every military
endeavor in the United Kingdom and the United States.
Under the direction of men such as P. M. S. Blackett
and Philip M. Morse, OR groups developed methodologies
and theories which were to transcend the immediate
military problems that they had been designed to
handle. Problems that were traditionally considered
intractable were made manageable by interdisciplinary
OR teams.

The following ten steps were developed, in
Chapter III, as the philosophical and methodological
foundations of virtually all OR studies:

1. The observations and study of the system's
   functions and operations.
2. The determination, definition, and delimitation
   of the system's problems.
3. The selection of the system's variables that are
   to be controlled, measured, and traded-off.
4. The establishment of measurement criteria, and
   subjective considerations of the system's
   variables, and uncertainties.

5. The collection and analysis of the system's data.

6. The search for appropriate model representations of the system.

7. The manipulation of the model representations so as to obtain optimum system trade-offs.

8. The examination of the accuracy, and the practicality of the system optimums derived from the models.

9. The communication and implementation of the model optimums into the system.

10. The reevaluation and adjustment of the implemented optimums through regular system monitoring and feedback analysis.

The necessity for all of the preceding steps in an OR study was explained in Chapter III. First hand observation is often the only way of obtaining an objective view of the system's operations. The proper statement of the system's problem often expedites the solution of the problem itself. The selection of variables involves finding appropriate trade-offs in order to reduce the number of variables to a manageable level without thereby losing the identity of the system under study. The measurement of variables requires criteria that are easily handled, yet sensitive enough to be compatible with the problem objectives. The analyses of data can be accomplished by any appropriate procedures without regard to the theoretical purity of the techniques used. The test of a model's appropriateness is determined by the degree to which the model simplifies and predicts the behavior of the original system while simultaneously maintaining its identity. The manipulation of these models by a relatively new battery of optimization techniques represents the principal uniqueness of OR studies as compared to the more traditional scientific methods. Optimal solutions derived from models must be tested for accuracy and practicality before being accepted as solutions to system problems. The OR solution of a system problem is intimately tied to the implementation, and the communication of that solution to those who are charged with operating the system. Finally, since optimal solutions are functions of circumstance, systems have to be constantly monitored so as to reevaluate and readjust model representations and operating optimums to changing inputs and conditions.

All disciplines are subject to pitfalls and fallacies in the application of their techniques. As demonstrated in Chapter IV, OR is especially vulnerable to pitfalls and fallacies because it is relatively new, and thus many of its procedures are not properly codified. Pitfalls and fallacies may arise due to superficial studies which fail to gather complete data, or fail to consider all aspects of the problem. They may also arise due to improperly trained OR groups who fail to consult system personnel, or fail to consider the human aspects of the problem. One of the most prevalent fallacies revolves around the suboptimization of a system which can lead to accepting, mistakenly, the combined optimums of the system's components as the overall system optimum. A prevalent pitfall involves the assumption of the independence of events, when in fact, most events are highly inter-dependent. The imposition of static OR techniques on dynamic system problems can lead to still another OR pitfall based on the incompatibility of the model with the system problem. Finally, fallacies can arise in OR studies due to an overreliance on abstract mathematical models and techniques which bear little resemblance to the realities of the actual system, but are used because of the ease with which optimum solutions can be derived from them.

In Chapter V, the concept and nature of modeling was defined, developed, and demonstrated to be central to the study of OR. The attempt to adapt

the mathematical models of the natural sciences,
developed up to the nineteenth centry, to the
operational sciences of the twentieth century was
doomed to be unsuccessful because the natural science
models were too simple, their variables too streamlined, their assumptions too generous, their formulations too skimpy, and their methods too inadequate
to deal with the magnitude and dynamics of complex
system problems. The unique models of OR were
devised to meet these inadequacies, just as Newton
had to develop the calculus in order to handle problems
that were not amenable to the mathematical models
of his day. The development of models appropriate
for the social sciences is still in the formative
stages, but the preliminary modeling has relied
heavily on a combination of the classical natural
science models, along with an increasingly heavy
emphasis on OR model constructs.

OR models may be conveniently classified into
two broad classifications -- qualitative and quantitative. The qualitative models are basically descriptive in nature, and generally cannot be used to
predict or improve system outcomes. The quantitative
models on the other hand, are specifically designed
to handle one or more types of system problems, and
normally can be expected to yield analyses on how

to predict and improve system operations, or at the very least, to identify which aspect of the system requires improvement.

Qualitative models such as formula, black-box, Venn diagram, and flow chart models were discussed in Chapter V, and applied to the CJ system. A formula used by forensic scientists to determine the time of death of a corpse was explained. Another formula showed the relationships between the generation and prevention of crimes. A new formula was developed in this study that related the total number of potential n-tuple crime interactions as a function of the number of persons in the society. Black-box models treated as input-output systems with feedback loops were applied to the classroom teaching situation, the use of forensic science equipment, the rehabilitation of convicted criminals, and the utilization of a city's law enforcement resources. Venn diagrams considered as intersections and unions of related sets, were applied to calls for police service, to societal interactions, criminal activities, and court jurisdictions. Quantified flow charts, used to demonstrate system functioning, were developed to illustrate the processing of felony cases, and crime victimization versus criminal conviction rates. In addition, a flow chart was

displayed that showed all the intricate relationships within the CJ system.

The assignment algorithm provides an optimal
method for allocating resources to destinations,
provided a standard measurement criterion is known
between all the points of resource and destination.
A brief historical sketch of the algorithm's development was provided in Chapter VI. A complete and
expanded version of the Hungarian method for solving
the assignment problem was presented which included
specific steps for determining the minimum number
of covering lines, and for determining alternate
optimal solutions. There has been no prior application of the assignment algorithm to the problems
of the CJ system. The algorithm was demonstrated
by introducing a problem typical in the administration
of a forensic science laboratory. A method for
applying any arbitrary number of weighted measurement
criteria to the assignment of resources to destinations was developed in this study.

The transportation algorithm involves the optimal
allocation of given quantities of supplies from sources
to destinations with associated demands, provided a
standard measurement criterion is known between each
point of source and destination. A brief historical
sketch of the problem's origin was discussed. A new

inequality was presented in this study in Chapter VII,
that provides a measure for the maximum total number
of possible allocations in a given transportation
problem. A modified and improved form of the algorithm
developed by William R. Vogel was presented, which
provides for a nearly optimal initial solution, and
demonstrates an iterative test for optimality. There
has been no prior application of the algorithm to the
problems of the CJ system. Applications of the
transportation algorithm to the transfer of inmates
between institutions, and the refueling of motorized
police units were presented. A method was demonstrated
in this study that allows for the listing of all
alternatively optimal solutions for a given transportation problem.

The problem of sequencing involves the ordering
of multistage jobs of known processing times, so as
to provide the minimum total downtime or delay during
the processing operation. A brief historical sketch
of the algorithm, which is currently limited to
two-stage and some three-stage processing jobs, was
presented in Chapter VIII. The S. M. Johnson algorithm
was outlined, and modified to display alternate optimal
solutions which permit greater sequencing flexibility.
The algorithm was applied to a problem in the forensic
science investigation and documentation of evidence.

There has been no previous application of the algorithm to the problems of the CJ system. An original algorithm was developed in this study that allows for most or all of the downtime to be concentrated at the beginning of the second stage, so that the second stage can be processed with a minimum of interruption once its processing is begun. The three-stage Johnson algorithm was applied to the preparation of cases for trial by the District Attorney's Office. In the three-stage sequencing problem, an original algorithm provided for a minimum of interruption at stage three, and which also allowed a minor improvement in the gaps of the second-stage processing sequence.

A queue exists whenever there are customers waiting to use facilities, and in some instances when there are idle facilities without customers. The basic M/M/C queueing model was presented in Chapter IX, along with a brief sketch of the literature that described its use in the CJ system. Formulas for the M/M/C queueing model were presented and applied to the trial queue in a typical criminal court system. The study showed that a criminal court jurisdiction had a .99 utilization factor, and since this high utilization factor is typical for many court systems it indicated that many municipal court operations are in danger of total collapse. A .85 utilization factor is a typical threshold danger value involving machine operation queues. A .70 utilization factor was conjectured to be the highest value permissible for operations involving human activities, yet most CJ operations are regularly operating above the .90 utilization level. However, unilateral reductions in danger-zone operations for any one unit of the CJ system cannot be accomplished by providing increased services in that unit alone. Such an approach would lead to a potential sub-optimization fallacy. The only suitable method to reduce danger-zone operations must involve the optimal balance of additional resources among all the units of the CJ system.

The method of simultation is required quite frequently in seeking optimal solutions to the problems of dynamic systems such as the CJ system, particularly when the model and data constructs are both probabilistic in nature. An historical sketch of the origins of simulation, and the reasons for its use was provided in Chapter X. A brief sketch of the literature that involved the use of simulation methods in the study of the CJ system was provided. The two basic computer languages used for simulation problems are SIMSCRIPT and GPSS.

The hand method of simulation known as Monte Carlo was discussed and with the aid of a table of random digits, a simulation was run on the effects of combining three existing police precincts into various combinations of proposed new precincts. The simulation was based on the existing frequency data for the incoming calls for police service at the three existing precincts. It must be emphasized that the accuracy of the simulation runs depended directly on the accuracy of these initial frequency data. The results demonstrated that due to the fact that the incoming calls were basically stochastic, a simple averaging model of the existing precinct frequency distributions would be generally misleading, and usually inaccurate in any predictive model formulation for the behavior of the new precincts. The study developed graphs and tables based on the simulation runs to illustrate the predicted call intervals at the proposed new police precincts.

Up to the present, there has been relatively little application of the mathematical models of OR to the problems of the CJ system. This work has attempted to bridge the communication gap between OR and CJ professionals in order to increase the use of OR models in the solution of CJ system problems.

The methods of OR, historically successful in the
fields of business, economics, industry, and warfare,
provide great promise for improving the operations
of the CJ system. However, the CJ system is a far
more complicated system than any of the others
previously subjected to OR analyses. Consequently,
advances and improvements in the CJ system due to
OR will probably evolve slowly and imperceptively
for sometime to come, especially since professionals
from both disciplines still eye each other with
some degree of caution and suspicion. At present,
the main OR techniques employed to study the CJ
system have been flow charts, queueing theory and
simulation. As this work has tried to indicate,
there are still many fertile areas in CJ that are
amenable to OR methods that, as yet, have gone
unnoticed, or unexplored.

Some unapplied OR methods to the problems of the
CJ system that merit further study include, the application of information theory models to forensic science,
the application of graphical linear programming to
police resource allocation, the application of
statistical and probability analyses to the police
post hazard plan, the application of integer and
quadratic programming methods to purchase and budget
problems of CJ departments, the application of

coordination methods such as PERT and CPM to the analyses of planning CJ contracts, grants, and projects, the application of game and decision theory to curb organized crime, and the application of search theory to uncover illegal drug activities.

Some other areas of the CJ system that seem appropriate for OR studies include the operations of the special investigative units, the organization of the jury system, the purchasing of special equipment, the scheduling of court calendars, the assignment of parole, the sentencing of convicted criminals, the classification of laws and penalties, the adminstration of prisons, the rehabilitation of convicts, the assignment of accused perpetrators to special treatment centers, the reduction of time from arrest to sentencing, the coordination of departmental statistical data, the effects of more efficient CJ services on the crime rates, the readjustment of released prisoners to society, the allocation of detective squads, and the optimal blend of uniformed and non-uniformed law enforcement patrols.

This work has attempted to provide the background, incentive, and the knowledge for educators and practitioners in both OR and CJ to take up the challenge, and tackle some of the many problems

of the CJ system, the solutions to which promise
to improve the system, aid society, and permit
former criminals to become productive citizens.
Undoubtedly, the energies and the talents that
will go into these future studies may produce
newer and better model representations of value
to both the OR and the CJ professionals, as well
as to society in general.

BIBLIOGRAPHY

Abrams, John W. "Implementation of Operational Research: A Problem in Sociology." Journal of the Canadian Operational Research Society, 3 (November, 1965), 152-160.

Ackoff, Russell L. "The Development of Operations Research as a Science." Operations Research, 4 (June, 1956), 265-295.

_____. ed. Progress in Operations Research, Vol. I. New York: John Wiley & Sons, Inc., 1966.

_____, and Rivett, Patrick. A Manager's Guide to Operations Research. New York: John Wiley & Sons, Inc., 1967.

_____, and Sasieni, Maurice W. Fundamentals of Operations Research. New York: John Wiley & Sons, Inc., 1968.

Allocation of Patrol Manpower Resources in the Saint Louis Police Department, 2 Vols. (An experiment conducted under the Office of Law Enforcement, Grant No. 39.) Thomas McEwen, Project Director. St. Louis, Mo.: St. Louis Police Department, July, 1966.

Aristotle On Man in the Universe. Edited by Louise R. Loomis. New York: Walter J. Black, 1943.

Baker, James D. "On the Criminal Justice System." Law Enforcement Science and Technology II. Edited by S. I. Cohn. Chicago: IIT Research Institute, 1969.

Ball, W. W. R. Mathematical Recreations and Essays, 11th Edition. Revised by H. S. M. Coxeter. New York: The Macmillan Co., 1939.

Beer, Stafford. Decision and Control. London: John Wiley & Sons, Inc., 1966.

Benecke, Theodore. "Methods of Air Defence Over Germany in World War II." Operational Research in Practice. Edited by Max Davies and Michel Verhulst. London: Pergamon Press, 1958.

- 249 -

Blackett, P. M. S. "Operational Research." The Advancement of Science, V (April, 1948), 26-38.

Blumstein, Alfred. "Outline of a Future Research and Development Program." Law Enforcement Science and Technology II. Edited by S. I. Cohn. Chicago: IIT Research Institute, 1969.

_____ and Larson, Richard. "Models of a Total Criminal Justice System." Operations Research, 17 (March-April, 1969), 219-232.

Bohigian, Haig. "OR Education for Criminal Justice Professionals." Paper presented at the 38th national meeting of the Operations Research Society of America, Detroit, Mich., October 30, 1970.

Bonder, Seth. "Needs in Operations Research Education." Paper presented at the 37th national meeting of the Operations Research Society of America, Washington, D. C., April 22, 1970.

Boyer, Carl B. A History of Mathematics. New York: John Wiley & Sons, Inc., 1968.

Brockmeyer, E.; Halstrom, H. L.; and Jensen, Arne. "The Life and Works of A. K. Erlang." Transactions of the Danish Academy of Technical Sciences, 2 (1948), 16-18.

Chamberlin, Roy B. and Feldman, Herman. The Dartmouth Bible. 2nd. ed. Boston: Houghton Mifflin Co., 1961.

Charnes, A. and Cooper, W. W. "The Stepping Stone Method of Explaining Linear Programming Calculations in Transportation Problems." Management Science, 1 (October, 1954), 49-69.

_____. "Such Solutions Are Very Little Solved." Operations Research, 3 (August, 1955), 345-346.

Chorafas, Dimitris N. Systems and Simulation. New York: Academic Press, 1965.

Churchman, C. West; Ackoff, Russell L.; and Arnoff, E. Leonard. Introduction to Operations Research. New York: John Wiley & Sons, Inc., 1961.

- 250-

Cohn, S. I., ed. Law Enforcement Science and
    Technology II. Proceedings of the Second
    National Symposium on Law Enforcement
    Science and Technology. Chicago: IIT
    Research Institute, 1969.

Complete Writings of Thucydides: The Peloponnesian
    War. Translated by R. Crawley. New York:
    The Modern Library, 1934.

Cooper, Leon and Steinberg, David. Introduction to
    Methods of Optimization. Philadelphia:
    W. B. Saunders Co., 1970.

Cowan, Thomas A. "Social Implications of Operations
    Research." Operations Research, 3 (August,
    1955), 341-343.

Creelman, George D. and Wallen, Richard W. "The Place
    of Psychology in Operations Research."
    Operations Research, 6 (January-February, 1958),
    116-121.

Crowther, J. G. and Whiddington, R. Science at War.
    New York: Philosophical Library, 1948.

Dantzig, George B. "Application of the Simplex Method
    to a Transportation Problem." Activity Analysis
    of Production and Allocation. Edited by
    T. C. Koopmans. New York: John Wiley & Sons,
    Inc., 1951.

_____. "Discrete-Variable Extremum Problems."
    Operations Research, 5 (April, 1957), 266-276.

_____, Fulkerson, D. R. and Johnson, S. M. "Solutions
    of a Large-Scale Traveling-Salesman Problem."
    Operations Research, 2 (November-December, 1954),
    393-410.

Davies, Handel, and Silman, K. E. "Some Examples of
    Systems Analysis." Operational Research in
    Practice. Edited by Max Davies and Michel
    Verhulst. London: Pergamon Press, 1958.

Davies, Max, and Verhulst, Michel, eds. Operational
    Research in Practice. London: Pergamon Press,
    1958.

Day, Frank D. "Administration of Criminal Justice:
An Educational Design in Higher Education."
Journal of Criminal Law, Criminology, and
Police Science, 56 (December, 1965), 540-544.

Egervary, E. "Matrixok Kombinatorikus Tulajdonsa-
gairól." Matematikai es Fizikai Lapok, 38
(1931), 16-28.

Ellis, H. F. "Written in a Queue." Operations
Research, 6 (January-February, 1958), 125-127.

Ennis, Philip H. "The Measurement of Crime in the
United States." Law Enforcement Science
and Technology I. Edited by S. A. Yefsky.
Washington, D. C.: Thompson Book Co., 1967.

Flood, Merrill M. "The Traveling-Salesman Problem."
Operations Research, 4 (January-February, 1956),
61-75.

Ford, L. R. and Fulkerson, D. R. "Solving the Transportation Problem." Management Science, 3
(1956), 24-32.

Frobenius, F. Georg. "Uber Matrizen aus Nicht
Negativen Elementen." Sitzungsberitche,
Berliner Akademie, 23 (1912), 456-477.

Gass, Saul I. "On the Division of Police Districts
into Patrol Beats." Proceedings of the 23rd
National Conference. Association for Comput-
ing Machinery. Princeton, N. J.: Brandon/
Systems Press, Inc., 1968.

Germann, A. C. "Education and Professional Law
Enforcement." Journal of Criminal Law,
Criminology, and Police Science, 58
(June, 1967), 603-609.

Giffler, B., and Thompson, G. L. "Algorithms for
Solving Production-Scheduling Problems."
Operations Research, 8 (July-August, 1960),
487-503.

Gödel, Kurt. On Undecidable Propositions of Formal
Mathematical Systems. Princeton: Princeton
University Press, 1934.

Goodeve, Sir Charles. "Operational Research."
Nature, 161 (March 13, 1948), 377-384.

Greenberg, Irwin. "A New Application of Operations Research." Operations Research, 8 (May-June, 1960), 423-424.

Greenwood, Peter W. An Analysis of the Apprehension Activities of the New York City Police Department. RAND Report R-529-NYC. New York: The New York City RAND Institute, September, 1970.

Halsburg, Earl of. "From Plato to the Linear Program." Operations Research, 3 (August, 1955), 234-254.

Hauser, Norbert; Gordon, Gilbert R.; and Surkis, Julius. Computer Simulation of a Police Emergency Response System. (A report prepared for the Law Enforcement Administration of the United States Department of Justice, Project No. 030.) New York: Polytechnic Institute of Brooklyn, September, 1969.

Heller, J. "Some Numerical Experiments for an M × J Flow Shop and Its Decision-Theoretical Aspects." Operations Research, 8 (March-April, 1960), 178-184.

Heller, Nelson B. "Proportional Rotating Schedules." Unpublished Ph.D. dissertation, University of Pennsylvania, 1969.

_____ and Kolde, Richard. "The Use of Simulation in Planning Expansion of the St. Louis Police Real-Time Motor Vehicle Inquiry System." Paper presented at the 38th national meeting of the Operations Research Society of America, Detroit, Michigan, October 30, 1970.

_____ and Markland, Robert E. "A Climatological Model for Forecasting the Demand for Police Service." Paper presented at the 37th national meeting of the Operations Research Society of America, Washington, D. C., April 20, 1970.

Helmer, Olaf and Rescher, Nicholas. "On the Epistemology of the Inexact Sciences." Management Science, 6 (October, 1959), 25-52.

Herrmann, William W. "Public Order in a Free Society: A Problem in Suboptimization." Law Enforcement Science and Technology II. Edited by S. I. Cohn, Chicago: IIT Research Institute, 1969.

Herskala, Victor H. "The Role of O. R. Techniques in the Army." Paper presented at the 35th national meeting of the Operations Research Society of America, Denver, Colorado, June 17, 1969.

Hertz, David B. and Melese, Jacques, eds. Proceedings of the Fourth International Conference on Operational Research. New York: Wiley-Interscience, 1966.

Hillier, Frederick S., and Lieberman, Gerald. Introduction to Operations Research. San Francisco: Holden-Day, Inc., 1968.

Hitch, Charles. "An Appreciation of Systems Analysis." Operations Research, 3 (November, 1955), 466-481.

_____. "Comments." Operations Research, 4 (August, 1956), 426-430.

_____. "Uncertainties in Operations Research." Operations Research, 8 (July-August, 1960), 437-445.

_____, and McKean, Roland. "Suboptimization in Operations Research." Operations Research for Management. Vol. I. Edited by J. F. McCloskey and F. N. Trefethen. Baltimore: The John Hopkins Press, 1966.

Hitchcock, Frank L. "The Distribution of a Product from Several Sources to Numerous Localities." Journal of Mathematics and Physics, 20 (1941), 224-230.

Hoagbin, J., notes. Operations Research. Ann Arbor: The University of Michigan Press, 1957.

Hoover, J. Edgar. Uniform Crime Reports for the United States -- 1969. Washington, D. C.: Government Printing Office, 1970.

Hopkins, Nigel J. "Operations Research in Relation to the Human-Enterprise Process." Operations Research, 4 (June, 1956), 357-360.

Huff, Darrell. How to Lie With Statistics. New York: W. W. Norton & Co., Inc., 1954.

Hurni, M. L. "Observations on Operations Research."
Operations Research, 2 (August, 1954),
234-248.

Hypher, R. P. "Letter to the Editor." Operations
Research, 11 (January-February, 1958), 154-156.

Institute for Defense Analyses. Task Force Report:
The Courts. (A report to the President's
Commission on Law Enforcement and the Adminis-
tration of Justice.) Washington, D. C.:
Government Printing Office, 1967.

_____. Task Force Report: Science and Technology.
(A report to the President's Commission on
Law Enforcement and the Administration of
Justice.) Washington, D. C.: Government
Printing Office, 1967.

International Business Machine Corporation. General
Purpose Systems Simulator II. Reference Manual
B20-6346-1, Poughkeepsie, N. Y.: IBM Data
Processing Division, 1963.

Jennings, John B. The Flow of Defendants Through
the New York City Criminal Court in 1967.
RAND Report RM-6364-NYC. New York: The
New York City Rand Institute, September, 1970.

Jensen, Arne. "Safety-at-Sea Problems." Proceedings
of the Fourth International Conference on
Operational Research. Edited by D. B. Hertz
and J. Melese. New York: Wiley-Interscience,
1966.

Jessop, William N. "Operational Research Methods;
What are They?" Operational Research Quarterly,
7 (June, 1956), 49-58.

Johnson, Ellis A. "The Executive, the Organization,
and Operations Research." Operations Research
for Management. Vol. I. Edited by J. F.
McCloskey and F. N. Trefethen. Baltimore:
The Johns Hopkins Press, 1966.

_____. "The Long-Range Future of Operational
Research." Operations Research, 8 (January-
February, 1960), 1-23.

Johnson, W. T. M. "Why Operations Research?" Operations Research, 3 (February, 1955), 103-104.

Johnson, S. M. "Optimal Two and Three Stage Produc-
    tion Schedules with Setup Times Included."
    Naval Research Logistics Quarterly, 1 (1954),
    61-68.

Jourdain, Philip E. B. "The Nature of Mathematics."
    The World of Mathematics, Vol. I, Notes and
    comments by James R. Newman, New York:
    Simon and Schuster, 1956.

Kantorovitch, L. "On the Translocation of Masses."
    Management Science, 5 (October, 1958), 1-4.

Kendall, M. G. "The Teaching of Operational Research."
    Operational Research Quarterly, 9 (December,
    1968), 265-278.

King, William R. "On the Nature and Form of Operations
    Research." Operations Research, 15 (November-
    December, 1967), 1177-1180.

Kingston, Charles R. "Probability and Legal Proceed-
    ings." The Journal of Criminal Law, Criminology
    and Police Science, 57 (March, 1966), 93-98.

Kittel, Sir Charles. "The Nature and Development of
    Operations Research." Science, 105 (February 7,
    1947), 150-153.

Kline, Morris. Mathematics and the Physical World.
    New York: Thomas Y. Crowell, 1959.

König, Denes. "Uber Graphen und ihre Anwendung auf
    Determinatentheorie und Mengenlehre."
    Mathematische Annalen, 77 (1916), 453-465.

Koopman, B. O. "Fallacies in Operations Research."
    Operations Research, 4 (August, 1956), 422-426.

Koopmans, Tjalling C. "Optimum Utilization of the
    Transportation System." Econometrica, Vol. 17
    Supplement (July, 1949), 136-146.

Kuhn, H. W. "The Hungarian Metod for the Assignment
    Problem." Naval Research Logistics Quarterly,
    2 (1955), 83-97.

Lanchester, Frederick W. "Mathematics in Warfare."
    The World of Mathematics. Vol. 4. Notes
    and comments by J. R. Newman. New York:
    Simon and Schuster, 1956.

Larson, Richard C. _Models for the Allocation of Urban Police Patrol Forces_. Technical Report No. 44 Cambridge, Massachusetts: Massachusetts Institute of Technology, Operations Research Center, 1969.

_____. _Operational Study of the Police Response Time_. Technical Report No. 26. Cambridge, Massachusetts: Massachusetts Institute of Technology, Operations Research Center, 1967.

Levinson, Horace C. "Experiences in Commercial Operations Research." _Operations Research for Management_. Vol. I. Edited by J. F. McCloskey and F. N. Trefethen. Baltimore: The Johns Hopkins Press, 1966.

Levin, Richard I. and Kirkpatrick, C. A. _Quantitative Approaches to Management_. New York: McGraw-Hill Book Co., 1965.

McCloskey, Joseph F. "Of Horseless Carriages, Flying Machines, and Operations Research." _Operations Research_, 4 (April, 1956), 141-147.

_____. "The Training for Operations Research." _Operations Research_. Notes by J. Hoagbin. Ann Arbor: The University of Michigan Press, 1957.

_____ and Trefethen, Florence N. eds. _Operations Research for Management_. Vol. I. Baltimore: The Johns Hopkins Press, 1966.

Margenau, Henry. "The Competence and Limitations of Scientific Method." _Operations Research_, 3 (May, 1955), 135-146.

Markowitz, Harry; Hausner, Bernard; and Karr, Herbert W. _SIMSCRIPT: A Simulation Programming Language_. Englewood Cliffs, N. J.: Prentice-Hall, Inc., 1965.

Marshall, Byron O., Jr. "Queueing Theory." _Operations Research for Management_. Vol. I. Edited by J. F. McCloskey and F. N. Trefethen. Baltimore: The John Hopkins Press, 1966.

Mayne, J. W. "Operational Research and the Design of Experiments." _Operations Research_, 4 (February, 1956), 113-116.

"The Meaning and Function of Operational Research."
Operational Research in Practice. Edited by
Max Davies and Michel Verhulst. London:
Pergamon Press, 1958.

Meyer, Herbert, ed. Symposium on Monte Carlo Methods.
New York: John Wiley & Sons, Inc., 1956.

Miller, David W. and Starr, Martin K. Executive
Decisions and Operations Research, 2nd ed.
Englewood Cliffs, N. J.: Prentice-Hall, Inc.,
1969.

Mood, Alex M. Review of Methods of Operations
Research, by Philip M. Morse and George E.
Kimball. Operations Research, 1 (November,
1953), 306-308.

_____. "Diversification of Operations Research."
Operations Research, 13 (March-April, 1965),
169-178.

_____. "Macro-Analysis of the American Educational
System." Operations Research, 17 (September-
October, 1969), 770-784.

_____. Private Communication. Letter dated
April 1, 1971.

Morganthalier, George W. "The Theory and Application
of Simulation in Operations Research." Progress
in Operations Research. Vol. I. Edited by
R. L. Ackoff. New York: John Wiley & Sons,
Inc., 1966.

Morris, Norval, "Crime Prevention and Professional
Education." Law Enforcement Science and
Technology I. Edited by S. A. Yefsky.
Washington, D. C.: Thompson Book Co., 1967.

Morse, Philip M. "The History and Development of
Operations Research." The Challenge to Systems
Analysis: Public Policy and Social Change,
Edited by J. Kelleher. New York: John Wiley
& Sons, Inc., 1970.

_____. "Operations Research - An Application of
the Scientific Method " The Technology Review,
55 (May, 1953), 2-8.

_____. "Operational Research in the Public Service."
Paper Presented at the Symposium on Operational
Research, sponsored by the Organisation for
Economic Co-Operation and Development, Dublin,
Ireland, September 29, 1965.

_____. Private Communication. Personal Interviews
on August 17 and 20, 1970.

_____. "Trends in Operations Research." Operations
Research, 1 (August, 1953), 159-165.

_____ and Kimball George E. Methods of Operations
Research. 1st ed. rev. Cambridge, Mass.:
The M.I.T. Press, 1970.

Navarro, Joseph A. and Taylor, Jean C. "Data Analyses
and Simulation of Court System in the District
of Columbia for the Processing of Felony
Defendants." Task Force Report: Science and
Technology. Institute for Defense Analyses.
Washington, D. C.: Government Printing Office,
1967.

Neumann, John von. "A Certain Zero-Sum Two-Person Game
Equivalent to the Optimal Assignment Problem."
John von Neumann: Collected Works, Vol. VI.
Edited by A. H. Taub. New York: The Macmillan
Co., 1963.

Newman, James R., notes and comments. The World of
Mathematics. 4 Vols. New York: Simon and
Schuster, 1956.

Olson, David G. "A Preventive Patrol Model." Paper
presented at the 37th national meeting of
the Operations Research Society of America,
Miami Beach, Florida, November 11, 1969.

Orden, Alex, "The Transhipment Problem." Management
Science, 2 (April, 1956), 276-285.

"Operational Research in the Research Associations."
Nature, 161 (April 17, 1948), 584-585.

"Operational Research in War and Peace." Nature, 160
(November 15, 1947), 660-662.

Pethel, Frank C. and Berilla, Donald. "A Communication
System for the Washington D. C. Police Depart-
ment." Law Enforcement Science and Technology I.
Edited by S. A. Yefsky. Washington, D. C.:
Thompson Book Co., 1967.

Pocock, J. W. "Operations Research and the Management Consultant." Operations Research, 1 (May, 1953), 137-144.

Plutarch "Marcellus." The World of Mathematics, Vol. I. Notes and Comments by J. R. Newman. New York: Simon and Schuster, 1956.

Raiffa, Howard. Decision Analysis. Reading, Mass.: Addison-Wesley Publishing Co., 1968.

RAND Corp. A Million Random Digits with 100,000 Normal Deviates. New York: The Free Press, 1955.

Randels, W. C. "Some Qualities to be Desired in Operations Research Personnel." Operations Research, 4 (February, 1956), 116-119.

Reinfeld, Nyles V. and Vogel, William R. Mathematical Programming. Englewood Cliffs, N. J.: Prentice-Hall, Inc., 1960.

Rich, R. P. "Simulation as an Aid in Model Building." Operations Research, 3 (February, 1955), 15-19.

Richmond, Samuel B. Operations Research for Management Decisions. New York: The Ronald Press Co., 1968.

Richtmyer, Robert D. and Neumann, John von. "Statistical Methods in Neutron Diffusion" John von Neumann: Collected Works, Vol. V. Edited by A. H. Taub. New York: The MacMillan Co., 1963.

Riddle, Donald H. "How Do You Educate Police? 'Like Anyone Else'." University Magazine, Princeton University, Spring, 1969 issue, 13-16.

Rinehart, Robert F. "Threats to the Growth of Operations Research in Business and Industry." Operations Research, 2 (August, 1954), 229-233.

Rivett, Patrick. An Introduction to Operations Research. New York: Basic Books, Inc., 1968.

Rizer, Conrad. "Police Mathematics." Unpublished Ed.D. dissertation, New York University, 1950.

Robinson, Julia. "On the Hamiltonian Game (A Traveling-Salesman Problem)." RAND Report RM-303. Santa Monica, Calif.: The RAND Institute, December 5, 1949.

Roy, Robert H. "An Outline for Research in Penology."
    Operations Research, 12 (January-February, 1964),
    1-15.

Saaty, Thomas L. Elements of Queueing Theory.
    New York: McGraw-Hill Book Co.., 1961.

_____. Mathematical Methods of Operations
    Research. New York: McGraw-Hill Book Co.,
    1959.

_____. Private Communication. Letter dated
    April 5, 1971.

Schneider, Erich. "Absatz Produktion und Lagerhaltung
    bei ein facher Produktion." Archiv für
    Mathematische Wirtschafts und Sozialforshung,
    4 (1938), 99-120.

Shumate, Robert P. and Crowther, Richard F.
    "Quantitative Methods for Optimizing the
    Allocation of Police Resources." Journal
    of Criminal Law, Criminology, and Police
    Science, 57 (June, 1966), 197-206.

Simon, Herbert A. and Newell, Allen. "Heuristic Problem
    Solving: The Next Advance in Operations
    Research." Operations Research, 6 (January-
    February, 1958), 1-10.

Singh, Jagjit. Great Ideas of Operations Research.
    New York: Dover Publications, Inc., 1968.

Sisson, Roger L. "Sequencing Theory." Progress
    in Operations Research. Vol. I. Edited by
    R. L. Ackoff. New York: John Wiley & Sons,
    Inc., 1966.

Smith, Dwight C. Jr., ed. NYSIIS: New York State
    Identification and Intelligence System:
    System Development Plan. Albany: New York
    State Executive Department, 1967.

Snow, Charles P. Science and Government. Cambridge,
    Mass.: Harvard University Press, 1961.

Solandt, Omond. "Observation, Experiment, and
    Measurement in Operations Research."
    Operations Research, 3 (February, 1955)
    1-14.

Speiden, Norman R. "Thomas A. Edison: Sketch of
    Activities, 1874-1881." Science, 105
    (February 7, 1947), 137-141.

Stillson, Paul. "Implementation of Problems in O.R."
Operations Research, 11 (January-February,
1963), 140-147.

Taub, A. H. ed. John von Neumann: Collected Works,
6 Vols. New York: The Macmillan Co., 1963.

Taylor, A. Hoyt. "Thomas A.Edison and the Naval
Research Laboratory." Science, 105 (February
7, 1947), 148-150.

Taylor, Frederick W. Scientific Management. 3rd ed.
New York: Harper and Brothers, 1947.

Thomas, Clayton J. "Military Gaming." Progress in
Operations Research. Vol. I. Edited by
R. L. Ackoff. New York: John Wiley & Sons
Inc., 1966.

Trefethen, Florence N. "A History of Operations
Research." Operations Research for Management.
Vol. I. Edited by J. F. McCloskey and
F. N. Trefethen. Baltimore: The Johns
Hopkins Press, 1966.

Waerden, B. L. van der. Science Awakening.
Translated by Arnold Dresden. New York:
John Wiley & Sons, Inc., 1963.

Wagner, Harvey M. "An Integer Linear Programming
Model for Machine Scheduling." Naval Research
Logistics Quarterly, 6 (1959), 131-140.

Wallace, William A. "Computer Simulation and Law
Enforcement: An Application to the Automobile
Theft Problem." Law Enforcement Science
and Technology I. Edited by S. A. Yefsky.
Washington, D. C.: Thompson Book Co., 1967.

Ware, Thomas M. "An Executive's Viewpoint."
Operations Research, 7 (January-February, 1959),
1-9.

Watson, Nelson A. "Police Philosophy: A Formula for
Crime." The Police Chief, XXXIV (September,
1967), 10-11,14,16.

Watson-Watt, Sir Robert. The Pulse of Radar (An
Autobiography). New York: The Dial Press, 1959.

_____. Three Steps to Victory. London, England:
Odhams Press, 1957.

Whitin, T. M. "Erich Schneider's Inventory Control Analysis." Operations Research, 2 (August, 1954), 329-334.

Whitmore, William F. "Edison and Operations Research." Operations Research, 1 (February, 1953), 83-85.

Williams, Eric C. "Reflections on Operations Research." Operations Research, 2 (November, 1954), 441-443.

Williams, Trevor I., ed. A Bibliographical Dictionary of Scientists. New York: Wiley-Interscience, 1969.

Willoughby, Stephen S. "Representations by Means of Formal Mathematical Structures." Unpublished Ed.D. dissertation, Columbia University, 1961.

Wilmer, M. A. P. "On the Measurement of Information in the Field of Criminal Detection." Operational Research Quarterly, 17 (December, 1966), 335-345.

Wooldridge, Dean E. "Operations Research -- The Scientists' Invasion of the Business World." The Journal of Industrial Engineering, VII (September-October, 1956), 230-235.

Yefsky, S. A. Law Enforcement Science and Technology I. Proceedings of the First National Symposium on Law Enforcement Science and Technology. Washington, D. C.: Thompson Book Co., 1967.

Zuckerman, Sir Solly. "The Need for Operational Research." Operational Research in Practice. Edited by Max Davies and Michel Verhulst. London: Pergamon Press, 1958.

NAME INDEX

Jethro, 13
Johnson, Ellis A., 12,28, 75,254
Johnson, S. M., 71,172,174, 176,179,182-185,187-189, 241,242,250,255
Johnson, W.T.M., 4,254
Joseph, Alexander, vi
Jourdain, Philip E.B., 15, 255

Kahn, Herman, 19
Kantorovitch, L., 150,255
Karr, Herbert W., 215,256
Kelleher, Grace, 2,257
Kendall, M. G., 2,50,255
Kepler, Johannes, 21
Kimball, George E., 4,47,52, 63,78-80,257,258
King, William R., 255
Kingston, Charles R., 86,255
Kirkpatrick, C. A., 25,26, 36,256
Kittel, Sir Charles, 4,5,255
Kline, Morris, vi,20,255
Kolde, Richard, 217,252
König, Denes, 129,255
Koopman, B. O., 92,93,255
Koopmans, Tjalling C., 150, 151,250,255
Kuhn, H. W., 129,255

Lanchester, Frederick W., viii,33-36,233,255
Larnder, G. H., 10,43
Larson, Richard C., 124,196 216,249,256

Lavoie, Edgar, vi
Levin, Richard I., 25,26, 36,256
Levine, Robert, vii
Levinson, Horace C., viii, 36-38,233,256
Lieberman, Gerald, 135,252
Livy (Titus Livius), 17
Loomis, Louise R., 248
Loughrey, Leo, vi
Lucian, 17

McCloskey, Joseph F., 11, 28,34-37,43,75,89,254,256, 261
McEwen, Thomas, 194,248
McKean, Roland, 89,90,252
Marcellus, 16,259
Margenau, Henry, 18,22,256
Markland, Robert E., 71,252
Markowitz, Harry, 215,256
Marshall, Bryon O., Jr., 28, 256
Mayne, J. W., 2,256
Melese, Jacques, 62,253,254
Mendel, Gregor J., 23
Mendelyeev, Dmitri I., 23
Meyer, Herbert, 214,257
Miller, David W., 26,134,257
Mood, Alex M., iii,76,79, 80,257
Morganthalier, George W., 214,257
Morris, Norval, iv, 257
Morse, Philip M., 2-4,8-10, 22,46-48,52,53,63,68,73, 78-80,231,234,257,258